!

Love,

Mana

2023

First paperback edition April 2021.

Edited by Beth Howe and Jordan Johnstone

Cover design and layout by Hannah Santi

ISBN # 9780578872025

GROWING UP

Navigating Life Between the Office and the Altar

In Christ,

Courtney

BY COURTNEY GRACE WATSON

ENDORSEMENTS

"Courtney's book is a refreshing reminder that we are called to live this life for Jesus and to be consistent whether at work, home, or somewhere in between."

-Kaitlin Chappell Rogers, author of *Not From God and Hey Little Flower Girl*

"As a young adult early in my career as a data developer, I deeply connect to each chapter in this book. From the feeling of imposter syndrome to the battle of comparison to the fear of failure, Courtney's words are a great reminder of how to navigate through life knowing my foundation and identity are in Christ."

-Madison Conant, Data Developer II at Ramsey Solutions

"The first time I met Courtney Watson, she was the token 20 something on a search taskforce interviewing me. She stood out, not only because of her age, but because of her wisdom and insight. Since that first meeting, I have been amazed to watch God work in her life. Whether writing a book, changing course in her career, or serving in the church, Courtney's love for Jesus and her commitment to trust Him isn't just something to say about her. It is her life's theme, born out of a crisis but now lived out each day. Like a modern day Esther, she understands that she is called for such a time as this. Her voice isn't one to be ignored or discounted. Rather, it is one that calls all of us to sit up, sit quietly, and to listen as God speaks through her. In *Growing Up: Navigating Life Between the Office and the Altar*, Courtney offers that same insight I witnessed when we first met. She reminds us that life and work require courage, wisdom, and perseverance. More importantly, Courtney's story and the lessons learned early in her career remind us that the source of all three is Jesus Christ."

-Pamela Hall, Minister to Women at Forest Hills Baptist Church

"For the working woman looking to gain wisdom, spiritual insight and stories of encouragement—Courtney's words inspire and express a story of how God works, redeems and guides us even in the midst of struggle in the workplace and in life. Every chapter has nuggets of practical and spiritual truths that will encourage you to press on and remember just who God made you to be!"

- Abby Williams, Development Manager for Narrow Gate Foundation

"*Growing Up* is a book that breathes life where our work breeds worry. With raw authenticity and bold truth-telling, Courtney steps alongside the woman who is at the start of something new and reminds her of who she is: A beloved daughter of the Almighty King who is called and equipped for this very moment. Where a thousand voices are shouting to chase the next thing, *Growing Up* is a call to stand where you are and see what the Lord has for you here before looking to where to go next. If you are beginning your career or changing paths along the way and feel overwhelmed with what to do now, you are in the right place."

- Joan L. Turley, author of *Sacred Work in Secular Place: Finding Joy in the Workplace—An Invitation to Partner With God in A Beautiful Broken World*

"*Growing Up* is the message we all need as we step into something new. If you are staring at the unknown, feeling the fear, and wondering how to face it with faith, Courtney invites you to grab a cup of coffee, sit right where you are, and find that you are not there alone. If you are leading young women in the early stages of their career, Courtney invites you to remember what it's like to feel uncertain and insecure in a new job position by sharing her own experiences and providing biblical examples of how to combat uncertainties. In any case, Courtney's vulnerability invites you to welcome your own in light of who God says you are."

- Csilla Muscan, speaker, author of *Dare To Awaken and Finding Your Voice*

For Meg and Annsley,

May we continue to grow up together.

TABLE OF CONTENTS

Foreword: *Diane Paddison, Founder and Executive Director of 4word. Author of "Work, Love, Pray" and "Be Refreshed"*

CHAPTER CONTENTS

FOREWORD

When Courtney Watson asked me to write the foreword for her book, *Growing Up: Navigating Life Between the Office and the Altar*, I couldn't wait to get started reading her book, as I knew she had recovered from a brain surgery and came out stronger. What or who made that happen?

Let me back up and share the background of our relationship.

I started 4word (www.4wordwomen.org) in 2011 and serve as the Executive Director, today, serving over 160,000 women in the workplace through our 4word Mentor Program with over 500 pairs graduating, 4word Community Groups meeting in thirty cities, and Digital Content reaching 160,000 in 2019. How did I have the platform and ability to do this? I was blessed, after growing up in a family fruit and vegetable business in Oregon, to go on to receive my Harvard MBA and become a global executive of two Fortune 500 companies and one Fortune 1000 company. Due to the fact that I was the only woman on those three global executive teams, as well as the 2010 Census data that factually proved that over 70% of women with children under eighteen were in the workplace and in over 40% of families the woman was the primary breadwinner, proved there was a need for a ministry like 4word.

It was through 4word that I met Courtney, as she leads our 4word: Nashville Community Group with other women in the workplace.

Our vision is to grow a global community of Christian women in the workplace so that we can help women reach their God-given potential with confidence, and Courtney exhibits this vision by writing her book. We value being real, authentic, and passionate about our work and strive to bring women in the workplace together in community.

Why did I leave those positions of influence and financial rewards to start and run 4word? I believe God strategically placed me in the workplace. He utilized the gifts and abilities I had there to provide a platform so that He could further accomplish His purpose in my life through 4word. Courtney lays out a similar story in this book as she was a Type-A driven woman in the workplace like me that God then interrupted. He used her horrible health situation for good. He clearly has a purpose for our lives…and He has a purpose for yours as well. God has a specific plan for your life and mine. When we trust in Him and walk closely with Him, He will open doors of opportunity for us we could never open on our own. Who would have thought a little farm girl from Oregon who went to the first eight grades of school in a four-room grade school would have the opportunity to go to Harvard Business School, be on three global executive teams, and lead a ministry for 160,000 women in the workplace? God must be at work.

In *Growing Up: Navigating Life Between the Office and the Altar,* Courtney shares how her focus changed when her brain surgery gave her a ten-week period of time to ponder while in recovery, "What was the Lord going to do with this?" How could she bring her work and her faith together?

God seems to know how to get our attention. For me it was a job loss due to my struggle around mismatched values versus my work environment. For Courtney, it was brain surgery. What will it take for you to understand that Jeremiah 29:11 is true? "For I know the plans I have for you, declares the Lord, plans to prosper you and not to harm you, plans to give you a hope and a future."

I am confident you will find this book inspirational and encouraging if you are entering the workplace, married to someone entering the workplace, or you are a parent or mentor of someone entering the workplace. I was captivated by the real story Courtney shares as she evaluated what God had planned for her... A must-read for everyone but especially those who have just entered the workplace.

May God use this book to help guide your life,

Diane Paddison

> Founder and Executive Director of 4word (www.4wordwomen.org). Author of *Work, Love, Pray* and *Be Refreshed . . . a year long devotional for women in the workplace.*
>
> Former Global Executive Team of two Fortune 500 and one Fortune 1000 companies (COO, Trammell Crow Company and ProLogis and President, Corporate Services, Client Accounts, CBRE)

A LETTER FROM THE AUTHOR

Hi, I'm Courtney!

I have no platform, no writing background, no husband, and no established career. Before you close this book and place it back on the shelf or close your Internet browser, I want you to know that I do have something: a message for you.

You may feel like you're drowning in expectations and to-do lists...

You may be struggling with fear and anxiety or comparison and control...

You may be trying to figure out how to navigate a life of faith in the working world...

My heart goes out to you, because I am right there with you. I'm just a young woman learning how to navigate life between the office and the altar. (See what I did there?)

I spent the first twenty-one years of my life working towards one goal: start a career. I worked hard in high school to get into college. I worked hard in college to get a good job. I got the good job... and then what? Sure, there are promotions to land and ladders to climb, but what was I supposed to do now that I had started my career? What do we do when we land our job and everybody shouts "Hooray!" as they push us out into the world to fend for ourselves like every other "adult?"

Naturally, I looked for the next thing, the next goal, the next step to work towards. But how do we look for the next thing when we don't even know how to hold the thing we see right now?

This was my biggest question when I first started working after graduating college. In an attempt to settle my mind and learn how to hold this new job in one hand while maintaining my relationship with the Lord and everyone else in my life in the other, I spent most of my free time reading books written by big-time executives and established professionals who absolutely knew what they were talking about. While these books offered valuable insight and knowledge, I always found myself at the final page thinking, "I appreciate their wisdom, but it's hard for me to relate to what they're saying. We are just on two very different ends of the spectrum."

Don't get me wrong. I would still encourage you to read books like *The Juggling Act* and *Work, Love, Pray* and *Every Good Endeavor*, but part of me always wanted someone to come beside me and just say, "I get it. You are not the only one struggling to keep your feet on solid ground. You're new to this, and that is okay. Breathe. You don't have to know your next step before you firmly land in this one."

That's why I wrote this book.

Already in my short professional life, I have experienced a health crisis that almost derailed the earliest days of my career, taken a step of faith by choosing to alter my career path, and written this book because of the overwhelming sense that I am not the only one struggling to navigate the world of work and the Word of God.

This book was born out of my health crisis, which I lovingly refer to as my "blessed fiasco," because it was there that my life was turned inside out and upside down and I discovered the blessing of being held personally by the very One who knit me together and knows every part of me. During that time, I also discovered that life is meant to be more than promotions and productivity.

The world is overrun with people telling us how to get to the top, how to make partner by thirty-five, how to be the best in our field, and how to become a CEO, but I don't often see people telling us how to work where we are in the beginning. There is nothing wrong with a healthy dose of ambition. Without a little ambition, you wouldn't be holding this book right now. The problem is that when we let our ambition become our end-all-be-all, telling us that we haven't "made it" until we reach the level of success our ambition deems worthy, we forget the beauty of where we are right now: spending our hours in a small cube in a dusty office with little view of the outside world.

The beauty is in the journey. It's waking up each day, putting in the work for whomever we work for, witnessing in our actions and our words that Jesus is Lord, declaring that all things—including us and our work—are *by* Him and *through* Him and *for* Him. It's recognizing that we may not be where we want to be, but we are a work in progress, just as much as our careers and relationships.

I'm so grateful you chose to read these words, whatever your reason. You are a prized possession to the King of kings, and I am honored that He might use these words to speak to you, His dearly loved child. God deserves every ounce of glory for this book because He is strong where we are weak. He is sovereign over even the smallest details affecting our lives.

My hope is that in these words, you will find that because you are known and seen and adopted by God, you do not have to prove yourself to be worthy or loved. You don't have to work your hands to the bone or your health to its breaking point to be a good worker because, in the work set before you today, God only requires obedience, not perfection. I hope you see that you are allowed to feel your fears, but you cannot let them dictate your decisions. I hope you see that you don't have to check your faith at the door of your office building, and you don't have to hide your profession as you enter the sanctuary, because God is working in both.

I hope you are reminded that God has created you for community, and you need people grounded in faith around you who are not only willing to celebrate the steps you take but are also ready to reach into the pit of despair and ease you out of darkness. I hope you find that even when jobs come and go, even when you've been waiting a while, even when people disappoint you and your work is hard, Jesus Christ stands firm as a foundation on which you build every part of your life.

I cannot promise eloquent words and powerful one-liners, but I can promise I will share with you what the Lord has shown me. I cannot give you the wisdom of professionals more than thirty years into their careers (though I have friends who have graciously offered a few words throughout the book), but I can open my heart and share with you the very same struggles you're facing now because I'm facing them as well.

I want to give you a space to feel like someone understands, like someone sees what's happening in your life right now. I can give you a sob story and a joke all on the same page if that is what it takes, because I want to partner with you in life. We are not meant to go through life alone. There will be struggles, friend, but take heart. We have each other, and more importantly, we have Jesus. May you meet Him here.

-Courtney

P.S. - I've included a "Chapter Zero" where I share more about my "blessed fiasco." I include this chapter because I believe it is a great testament to our God's ability to call us out of the depths of despair and into His marvelous light. Whether or not you read this chapter is entirely up to you, my friend. If you are struggling with something beyond the scope of this book that has you at your breaking point, I encourage you to read it and know that God sees you clearly and holds you closely just as He does for me. If you are just curious about how a CPA could end up writing a book, Chapter Zero will answer that question, too.

CHAPTER 0
The Blessed Fiasco

In August of 2017, I stepped into my first full-time job out of college. I had a fresh master's degree, three-fourths of a CPA license, and a pair of bright eyes that glowed at the thought of how life and work was going to go. I like to think I wasn't so naive that I didn't see any problems popping up along the way. I knew trials were inevitable in life, and I thought I knew how to look at a trial in front of me and shake my fist in triumph as I watched it bow to my God.

If I found myself working on a project I wasn't smart enough to complete on my own, I just *knew* the Lord would give me the knowledge to solve it.

If I found myself worrying about a situation happening in my family, I *knew* the Lord would make it all good.

If I found myself wondering how my life would look five years down the road, I *knew* the Lord's plan was for my best.

What I know now that I didn't know then is that these are all true. God will give us knowledge, but it may be found outside of ourselves and in a friend or mentor. God will make it all good but that does not mean it's good as it happens. God's plan for each of us is absolutely for our best, but our definition of "best" might look very different from God's.

I began to learn these lessons on a Monday afternoon, eight months into my career. In a matter of hours, I went from happily (as happily as one can be when working overtime hours in busy season) working on a tax return to almost stopping on the side of the interstate because I didn't think I could finish driving myself home. The months that followed are a blur, but they also provided clarity I didn't know I needed.

What I would learn a few weeks after that infamous day is that I have what's called a Chiari Malformation. Google it if you want but be warned, it's a scary thing and every time you get a headache from here on out you will have a nagging worry in the back of your mind that you have the same problem. (Or maybe that's just my worry.)

This condition is more common than you think. I don't say this to scare you. I say it to remove some of the fear and recognize that I am not the only one who has dealt with this problem. I say it to bring something I feared most into the light where it loses its power.

For eleven weeks, I lived without any reprieve from pain. I was overwhelmed with the thought that no one understood, no one knew what I was feeling or how excruciating the pain was, and no one could make this better. I don't want to turn this into a fight-for-yourself moment, but I do believe there are times when we need to push back when we're dismissed as being dramatic. In moments where we feel like no one understands us or believes us or wants to help us, we need to listen to our bodies and fight when they say fight. It wasn't until the fourth doctor and third MRI that I felt as though someone believed in my pain. Finding someone to listen and not dismiss your struggle is invaluable.

The day I found someone to listen, the pain didn't lessen, but I began to believe I could keep going as we fought to find healing together. For the next two months, we tried and we tried and we tried (fun fact - I can't taste Cokes when I take medicine for altitude sickness). After eleven weeks of not being able to sleep or eat or speak or really anything more than open my eyes and try my hardest to work through the pain, I found myself in a hospital bed signing papers that said I was cool with letting a doctor cut open my skull and if they needed another doctor to come in, I was cool with that, too.

Oddly enough, that second signature probably saved me that day, but that's another story. The story I want you to know is that even when you're laying in a hospital bed confirming that your affairs are in order should you not live to see the sunset, the Lord your God will not abandon you.

Thankfully, I survived the surgery that day and lived to tell the story. I also lived to spend the next two months in my dad's recliner eating ice cream cupcakes and saltine crackers. I think my parents are the real MVPs in all of this because despite the fact that my sister was getting married three weeks after my surgery, they rallied to help me do basically everything until I was strong enough to do things on my own again. And they thought their days of getting children in and out of bed and to the bathroom without an incident were behind them...

I think it's safe to say that summer did not go as I had anticipated. I had thought I would be in Nashville working towards a promotion, learning with my friends, gathering with my church family, and living my free-as-can-be life. My reality at the time was harsh... and it honestly still is. It's also the soil I needed to be planted in as I found myself hidden like a seed in the ground. There was no striving or working, only waiting and watching as the Lord tended to me in ways more personal than I thought possible.

For eleven weeks, I had been beaten down physically, mentally, spiritually, and emotionally, but I could finally see a light in all of my darkness. By the power of the Lord and through hundreds of prayers on my behalf, the relief was immediate.

And yet, the healing was slow. Just as I had been broken more than just physically, I needed to be bound back up in more ways than one. Where the relief happened quickly, I had to slowly work up to things like turning my head to either side, laying down and standing up without help, taking a step without a jarring feeling, walking around a store without needing a nap afterward, and putting my own shoes on. Talk about humble pie.

Beyond the physical, I struggled with finding purpose outside of work. I always thought I worked better in busyness. As I sat in recovery, I had nothing to do; no work to accomplish, no goal to work towards, and no challenge to think through. For the first time in as long as I could remember, I had no to-do list. Doubts related to what work would look like when I started back began piling up. I often questioned whether or not I would still be able to perform at the level I had in the past and whether or not people would treat me differently because I now had "brain surgery" written into my story.

I also struggled emotionally and spiritually as I found myself in the grips of depression. The pain I had experienced since that day in March made it difficult to laugh or cry or think or hope, and so I shut my emotions off in the name of self-preservation. I gave up trying to deal with the emotions I felt and quite honestly lost my desire to live. Depression is no joke, and while mine was more circumstantial than chemical, I still couldn't climb out of it on my own.[1] I thought I hid the depression well, but one of my aunts recognized it and swiftly enrolled me into what she called "Camp Katie," a week where she would force me to get up and moving, get out of the house, and ultimately reminded me what it felt like to *want* to live. Whether she knows it or not, Camp Katie changed the course of my recovery for this reason.

I won't say I gave up completely, but my moments of light were few and far between before the surgery. I struggled with seeing light and knowing joy when every morning I woke up with that same headache and pleaded for either relief or death. There were moments the Lord broke through my pain to remind me of His presence and His faithfulness and His worthiness to be praised, even in the midst of the hardest nights of my life. And so I sang, I cried, I spoke, I whispered, I silently thought the words in my mind nearly every day in the hope that even though I had nothing left, I would remember God with these words: *"Whatever's in front of me, help me to sing hallelujah..."*[2] These words, and more importantly the God who deserved my hallelujah, carried me through the darkness and into the view of light post-surgery. I still struggled and I still couldn't manage to pull myself from depression (Camp Katie to the rescue), but I could see the light and I could almost feel it.

Through the entire blessed fiasco, I was learning. I was learning about myself, my work, my faith, my God, and how all of that rolls into one life lived for one purpose: the glory of God.

I received what a mentor of mine called a "crash course in joy." That course involved breaking down walls, releasing expectations and life plans written in permanent ink, asking tough questions and sharing tense words with the God I was so angry with, and the unraveling of life as I knew it.

That course also involved meeting my Savior in the depths of despair, experiencing (for what felt like the first time) what it means to be loved by God when I was my most broken self, laying an empty planner into His hands, and finding the brightest view of hope and grace and strength that sustains in every day— even the ones you don't want to survive.

When all was said and done, the question that seemed to replay in my mind was, *"What are you going to do with what I've shown you?"*

The question echoed as I sat in a mountain of pillows with an ice pack wrapped around my head, as I sat behind the wheel of my car for the first time in two months, as I drove myself back home to Nashville and walked back into my office for the first time in ten weeks, and as I looked back and questioned why I had gone through this and how it could serve a purpose in my life. Even now, the question comes to mind as I replay the last few years of my life in both grief and gratitude.

I have lived a lot of life in twenty-five years. I have learned the power of a *Hallelujah* on a dark night. I have prayed for relief and at the same time picked one foot up to keep moving forward. I have found that faith in God, in His simultaneous goodness and sovereignty and faithfulness, is the glue that holds a person together when everything else screams *fall apart*. I have been shown greater glimpses of God than I could ever have hoped for, and I have learned lessons I never wanted to need. Through it all, God has given me a front-row seat to watch how He works, and it is a seat I do not take for granted. God has shown me how to build a life on Him, a life that includes my walk with Him and my professional career and my personal relationships all wrapped into one, and I intend to show the world what has been shown to me.

The years that followed my surgery have not been perfect by any means. I still struggle with how to work well when it seems mean-ingless, how to love people when I want to do the opposite, how to relinquish control into the hands of a loving God who knows what is for my best and His highest glory. I still need to be reminded that He sustains in suffering and in showers of good things alike. I still need to be reminded that any ounce of strength exists in me by His power and not by my own striving. I still need to be reminded that my work, my image, and my ability to measure up do not determine my worth. I still need to be reminded that God is good, even when life is not.

And I'm guessing you need these reminders too. Maybe one of them, maybe all of them.

I don't know what I did to deserve the privilege of sharing these words with you, but I will endeavor to share honestly and with a heart that is after the glory of only my Father. What I do know is that we all have stories of suffering and of success, and the Lord intends to use both for good.

CHAPTER 1
Start the Climb

"I don't like doing things I'm not good at," I said to my professor while going through my Master of Accountancy program.

His response? "Everything seems hard until you know how to do it."

The scary part is that every new thing we do is something we don't know how to do. That's the very nature of it. Starting a new job, beginning a new relationship, working on a new project, watching friends and family get married and have babies and knowing that marks a new season of friendship, just to name a few. The common thread? Change.

Every new thing means something has changed, whether for a season or a lifetime. I'm assuming that by picking up this book, you are at your very own beginning of something new. Stepping into a new workplace, walking the hallowed halls of your old high school except now you're the teacher, leaving what was comfortable for what is excitingly scary. Facing a new reality with a chronic illness, watching your workplace shift to a new culture you might not want to be part of, realizing a new season of singleness stretches before you. Whatever your situation, I'm glad you're here.

Much of this book is geared toward navigating a new professional season, but rest assured, the words can apply beyond the professional and into the intimately personal. That's the secret: navigating between the altar and the office is not just a catchy phrase. It's a lifelong pursuit of living one life, not living your work life and church life separately.

With that said, I'm with you, friend. I'm beginning this journey to write the very thing you now hold in your hands, and as excited as I am to do so and as loopy as the smile on my face looks as I sit here alone at a table for two, it's also terrifying. I don't feel qualified to write this book, just as you might not feel qualified or prepared to face what is before you now. Yet here we are. Doing something we're passionate about, squaring our shoulders in preparation to fight without letting our seeming lack of credibility stop us. As we dive into the reality of what it's like to be a young professional, a new business owner, or a new patient, may we step forward in faith, trusting that the God who brought us to this very moment will not leave us now.

As we both navigate this season of our lives, I want us to remember that we are new here. I walked into a new workplace for the first time and got lost in the stairwell, but it's okay because I'm new. I accidentally "replied all" to an email that included the entire firm, but it's okay because I'm new (and thankfully didn't say anything too embarrassing). I wrote for two hours and only came up with fifty usable words, but it's okay because I'm new (and writing is hard).

Our work is new to us, and so we don't know everything. You may be thinking, "Well duh!" On the other hand, maybe you're thinking, "Yeah, right, this college degree would tell you otherwise." But seriously, as much as we like to think we're going to rock this new thing, we need to know we're going to make mistakes along the way, especially in the beginning. We have to learn how to do this new thing before we can do it well.

During the first week of my first real job, I was told something along the lines of, "You likely don't know a lot about what you've just walked into. In fact, we assume you don't and that's why we're going to teach you." I don't know about y'all, but my quick-beating heart needed to hear those words during that first week when papers were signed that I didn't really understand and when managers kept talking about this Sally person I didn't even know (in case you didn't know, "SALY" is a short way of saying "same as last year").

If you're beginning a new job, your employer will teach you what you need to know to do your job, and not only will you be taught how to do your job, there's also a shift in how your performance is measured. If you're not prepared for this, buckle up, sister, because no longer will you receive an A on a test or a passing score in a class to know you're on track with your progress. These metrics are left behind after graduation and in their place are metrics unique to every workplace, all of which will be included in the learning curve you are about to experience. If you are anything like me and your plan is to walk in on Day One and be a straight-A worker, I want you to take a deep breath, remember this is new, and know that all you need to do on Day One is be honest in your understanding (or lack of understanding) and acknowledge you don't actually know it all but are ready to learn. A healthy dose of humility will go a long way here.

Yes, if you've been through the courses and taken the exams or worked your way up the ladder to this new position, you're expected to know the basics or else you wouldn't have been hired for the job, but it's no secret you don't know it all. And that is okay. It's more than okay because you're right where you're supposed to be. You are not alone in feeling overwhelmed by everything you don't know but feel like you should know. Every new job brings new challenges, new processes, new responsibilities, and new people into your life. No matter what, there is a learning curve. Even down to your very first job as a cashier or a waiter or, in my case, a car-washer. You walk in on the first day and while you know what the job is going to be, you don't really know how the boss wants the job done.

In my case, the boss was my dad and my Grandaddy, and they were very particular with how they wanted the job done. They had cars to sell or rent, and by gosh, those cars needed to look good. That's where I came in. At the ripe old age of ten, I was going to wash the cars and it was a big job opportunity for me because for every car I washed my Grandaddy gave me $2 and my dad gave me a house to live in and food to eat (kind of kidding, but seriously that was my payment in my dad's love-filled but business-minded eyes). All joking aside, I can remember times I would wash a car for my dad and he would come inspect the car and tell me the windows were streaky or the tires weren't clean enough, and then he would toss me the newspaper to rewash the window or the rag used to make the tires shine a little brighter. The first few cars I ended up cleaning again, but that was only because I had to learn how to do the job right.

My job as a CPA was really no different. The first few seasons were just one big learning curve. I had to learn the ins and outs of the software, the systems, and the processes my department used to prepare the tax returns. If things weren't done correctly the first time, the returns would be sent back to me to fix, sometimes with literal pages of corrections to make. Different job, same concept.

Life situations work much the same way. We get a new diagnosis and begin the curve of learning how to manage, how to live an abundant life even with underlying pain, how to work and laugh and maintain relationships when your reality is now different. We begin a new friendship and start learning how to communicate with this new friend, what they need from us and what we need from them, and how to be there for each other.

What is your new step in life? Think about it for a second. Have you already experienced a glimpse of this learning curve? If so, take a moment to think about the progress you've already made since Day One. You finally figured out how to get from the parking lot to your desk or office without getting lost - progress! You managed to get the IV in your patient's arm on the second try rather than the fourth - progress! You allowed yourself to ask a friend for help instead of trying to do it all on your own - progress!

If you haven't experienced this yet, let me be very clear: you will experience it sooner or later. After all, if we didn't have to rewash the windows or re-prepare the same return, would we ever truly learn? Would we grow in knowledge and wisdom without a few bumps along the road? I know it doesn't make the learning curve any easier to climb up, but maybe it will give you comfort in knowing this is not a problem unique to you. If you take a moment to look around you, you will see you are not alone in the climb. There are others climbing beside you. Some are ahead, some are behind, some are right on par, but we are all climbing. We are all growing up. One day, you will wake up, go to work, greet the next round of newbies, and realize how far you've come since you were in their shoes. That's the moment you'll reach back to help as those ahead did for you, but for now, get ready to climb.

We see this same learning curve throughout the Bible, except we call this maturing in our faith. We look at Moses, who didn't feel qualified to lead the Israelites out of Egypt. When the Lord first approached Moses with this task, Moses responded with doubt and protested four times about how unqualified he was before pleading a fifth time by saying "Lord, please! Send anyone else."[3] Through the plagues in Egypt, the deliverance out of Egypt, and the traveling in the desert for forty years, Moses faced many trials. The important thing to remember is that with each trial, Moses grew closer to the Lord, leaning into His presence more and more with every assignment. This doesn't mean Moses didn't fall short every now and then, but we see his faith maturing as he goes from the man who begged the Lord to send someone else to the man who said to the

Lord, "If you don't personally go with us, don't make us leave this place."[4] Moses had learned the value of the presence of the Lord. He had learned how capable he was to obey God's call when the Lord Himself went with him.

One thing I want to point out here is the Lord was preparing and equipping Moses with the tools he would need to be successful far before he was ever officially asked to lead the Israelites. Warren Wiersbe said it best: "Leading stubborn sheep was just the kind of preparation he needed for leading a nation of stubborn people."[5] Moses saw his years of being a shepherd in Midian as just an escape from punishment for killing an Egyptian, but God was preparing him for a role he knew nothing about. Even as Moses first led the Israelites, not knowing exactly how to do his new job and learning how best to lead the people, God knew Moses was capable of doing this job well, because God himself had prepared his way. Just as the Lord prepared Moses for his role, the Lord has prepared you for your new role. You still have to walk through the learning curve, but each step can be taken in confidence because the Lord Himself has equipped you and walks with you.[6]

We see this theme continuing in the New Testament as the disciples learned what it meant to share the Gospel when Jesus took them under his wing. Peter even cut off a man's ear only to have Jesus reattach it and essentially say, "Try that response again." Peter then denied Jesus three times. Jesus came back to him after the Resurrection as if to again say "Try that response again." Jesus asked Peter if he loved Him three times to which Peter, knowing better this time around, responded, "Yes, Lord, you know that I love you."[7]

Similar to the one you will see in your new role, your faith will also experience a learning curve. Colossians 2:6-7 (NLT) says, *"And now, just as you accepted Christ Jesus as your Lord, you must continue to follow him. Let your roots grow down into him, and let your lives be built on him. Then your faith will grow strong in the truth you were taught, and you will overflow with thankfulness."* I love the phrase "built on him." Your faith and your career both have to be built, and the best way to build is to build on Christ.

As a new believer, you know the foundation of salvation is Christ's death and resurrection reconciling us with God the Father, but there is so much more to learn about who God is, what God has done, who God says you are, and what He is calling you to do for Him. In the world of faith, this acknowledgment of your lack of understanding and need for help is celebrated because it's honest. As believers, we recognize the value of approaching the throne of God as a child, as someone who knows enough to be enthralled but not enough to understand every mystery of God. We embrace where we are right now, and we look to the sanctifying process of growing in Christ and becoming more like Him as we grow in our faith.

The same should be true of our work. We should embrace the fact that we are new and don't know a lot about what we need to be doing, and we start learning and building up our knowledge of the work we were hired to do. When you find yourself in your job saying, "Choose someone else because I can't do this!" like Moses or acting like Peter in essence (I sincerely hope you have not cut a man's ear off at work), know you are in good company. We all have moments where the learning has not fully taken root in our professional or spiritual lives, but even there, we have Jesus who covers us with grace and encourages us to try again.

In my personal experience, a large part of this process is being authentic. Be honest with yourself and those around you about where you are and what you need. This honesty might lead to more questions asked on the front-end, but you will grow exponentially when you stop trying to pretend you know what to do when you really don't.

Your potential will also grow as those around you see your openness and willingness to really understand how best to do your job because in all reality, that's what you're here for. You are here to do a job and do it well. So why not give up the "too cool for school" facade and admit when you need help? Those around you recognize your "new" status just as much as you do, and if you are entering a healthy space, they will be ready to help you. Accept the help and grow together, side by side. Growing together is much more fun than having to grow on your own.

As we go through this process of growing together and building up in Christ (me writing and you reading but both of us learning), I ask that you continue to remember the new. The new job, the new season, the new work the Lord is doing in your life. Embrace this time in your journey, because it's an opportunity to draw nearer to the throne of grace with confidence as you receive mercy and find the help you need. And now, in the new, before we really start climbing the learning curve, can we take a moment to celebrate?

AS YOU GROW UP: A LETTER FROM PATTY ROSS

With every new job comes new responsibilities and opportunities for growth.

One year after retiring from Nike, Inc., following a successful 34-year executive career, Apple hired me as an Executive Advisor for the People function at Apple headquarters, supporting its talent management, engagement, inclusion, and diversity strategies across all US and global divisions. While this was a big deal, and I was appreciative of this opportunity, deep down, I was not sure this was what I wanted. Never-the-less, I told myself why not, give it a try for a year and then decide what's next. So, I said yes, despite feeling a lot of mixed emotions, totally out of my comfort zone, unsettled, and yet optimistic.

The first week was challenging, and I felt lost...literally! On day one of driving on Apple Park's world headquarters, I went from not being able to find the right entrance into the campus, to my security badge not working, to creating a six-lane backup into the underground parking, to losing my car at the end of the day in the parking lot and needing security to drive me around in a golf cart to find it. And this was only the beginning of several humbling yet humorous moments where I found myself overwhelmed with doubt, regret, and asking myself what the heck am I doing?

While there were many more stories and situations to follow throughout this experience, through reflection, self-discovery, and God's grace, I found a heightened sense of inner strength, peace, confidence, and contentment that I have previously experienced. God provided me with exactly the tools I needed at just the right time.

What I know now, but didn't realize until later in my career, is that the evil one wants nothing more than for us to "play small." To lose sight of our God-given talents and gifts and instead question ourselves on whether or not we are good enough, which usually looks like questions like this:

- "What have I done?"

- "Do I have what it takes to advance my career?"

- "Did I handle that situation appropriately?"

- "Did I make the right decision?"

- "What will happen if I express what I want?"

- "What if I make a mistake?"

- "Am I able to have a successful career AND live a balanced, joyful, and fulfilling life?"

Do any of these questions sound familiar? What if I were to tell you that your self-doubt, insecurities and self-limiting beliefs are not from God, but come directly from the enemy, to kill, steal and destroy. How does that make you feel? For me, coming to this realization mid-career was a game-changer! How freeing to realize I had a choice on whether or not I was going to believe God or believe the lies of the enemy. I made a conscious and deliberate decision to no longer stuff and ignore my feelings, but instead wrap my arms around how I was feeling and bring that self-doubt, lack of confidence, and the question of self-worth to the cross. I started living and speaking a life based on God's promises versus others, which ignited a powerful transformation in my life.

A transformation that gave me the confidence to:

Know who I am and establish a sense of who I am as an integrated and whole person and to show up and live that consistently. To have a clear understanding of what is essential for my overall well-being. To know what I am willing to stand for relative to my priorities, my boundaries, and my non-negotiables.

Surround myself with strong role models, trusted partners, mentors, accountability partners. Truth-tellers, who enabled me to see my blind spots, to expand my perspective, to recognize my strengths, and to leverage the discipline and potential I never understood. To hold up the mirror so that I could objectively see myself for who I was – the areas of greatness as well as the areas where I was holding myself back.

Ignite purpose and fuel my passion. I began to dream, notice, and explore the things that evoked strong feelings and emotion in my life and looked for the unexpected and create possibilities of what could be and to expand my self-awareness and invest in my growth and development. I began to create transformational change in my life by having the courage to use my voice, follow my instinct, and not allow myself to play small.

So, I pray, as you're Growing Up, you would ponder these questions:

Who am I? When we become clear about who we are, what we value, what matters most, …others will then become apparent. So often, we do everything for everyone else at the expense of ourselves. And then we get frustrated and wonder why others don't see or value us.

Who do I want to be? We become what we believe. If we don't think we're good enough, that we should be at the table, that we have what it takes to do the job or get the promotion, then no one else will. Therefore, we need to pay close attention to how we talk to ourselves, how we support ourselves and be clear on where we're willing to invest our energy.

The analogy I like to use is the software updates on our computers. You know the "Updates Available" notification that shows up on our computers, the ones that we always choose the "remind me again tomorrow" option? When tomorrow arrives, we continue to delay again and again. We're too busy, we don't want to be interrupted, or maybe we're comfortable with how things are running right now. Then over time, our computers start running slower, laboring harder, struggling to perform. The updates didn't seem necessary at the time, but eventually, they do, which should make us wonder: why wouldn't we want to live every day with the capacity, power, and protection to be our authentic selves?

Do I mean it? The system sees you by what we feed it. Make sure your behaviors, actions, presence, and words support the vision of who you want to be. Invest in yourself, maintain boundaries, and use your voice. Focus on what you know feels right for you vs. other's perceptions. Let go of what is keeping you from stepping into your greatness. Be a light to those around you, for freedom happens when you no longer feel the need to prove, protect, or defend yourself.

CHAPTER 2
Celebrate the Now

Have you ever deep cleaned your house? Like really deep cleaned, the kind where you take a rag and run across every baseboard, empty out your closets, and move all your furniture to clean the places that *only* get cleaned when you do the deep clean? You work for hours to make your home feel clean and somehow new again, and then you sit down and enjoy the few minutes it actually stays that way before life once again brings the dust and clutter.

Think about those few minutes of calm. Maybe you labored for hours and you're so exhausted you can't think. Maybe you sit and look around at all you accomplished. Maybe you're already worrying about the next time you'll have to clean like this. Or maybe, like me, you revel in the project being done and celebrate with a nice long nap. I mean, if a day of rest was good for the Lord after creating the entire world in six days, an hour (or two) nap is good for me after deep cleaning the house in six hours....or more.

Now think about where you are right now. You've dedicated months or years to sit down at your own personal desk, to set up your very first classroom, or to meet your very first patient (human or canine). You've saved for what feels like a lifetime to afford your own car, house, or degree. You've battled illness and found yourself on the other side. You've packed your life up in boxes and moved across the country, state, or town. The moment is finally here. My hope is we all take time to revel in this beginning and to celebrate how we got here before rushing into the next thing on our to-do list or life plan. I hope we recognize the blood, sweat, tears, and prayers we put in to get where we are and praise the Lord for His hand in bringing us here. I hope we allow ourselves to be present in the newness and excitement of it all.

I think we all have a tendency to keep ourselves from celebrating the "normal" moments. We think everybody goes through this; everybody has to clean their house, people get jobs or houses or cars every day. Why should we celebrate this? Because God is here. He is bringing about this new thing in our lives because He is a good God who loves to give good gifts to His children. God was with us all along, filling us with knowledge to pass the exams, giving us courage to speak the truth and make the move, sustaining us when life got messy and it felt like there weren't enough hours in the day or strength in our bodies.

Every moment that God gives us the ability to pursue the purpose He planted deep within us is reason enough to celebrate. We will grow, but we must first appreciate—celebrate even—the planting. If someone else doesn't want to revel in receiving the gift of a new job, that's their business. But you and me? We are children of God, on the receiving end of a gift which not only allows us to put our talents and testimony into practice but allows us to step alongside the God of all creation and fulfill our purpose for the glory of His name. So let's celebrate these times.

One of the most well-known passages in the Bible is the story of God splitting the Red Sea in Exodus 14 and 15. At this point in history, the Israelites had been slaves in Egypt for 430 years and the Lord had chosen this moment to send Moses to rescue His people and lead them to the Promised Land. After the Israelites left Egypt, Pharaoh and the Egyptian army decided they wanted their workers back and they began to chase God's people all the way to the Red Sea.

Picture this: the people of Israel backed up against the Red Sea and the only humanly possible ways to escape were either to jump into the sea or run straight into the hands of the enemy. The human thought is immediately, "There is no way out. We left Egypt to be chased and cornered and killed here by the sea." And yet it was here, when their demise felt certain, that *the Lord parted the sea* and *provided a way* for His people. He rescued them...again. Then as if to make sure His people really understood how powerful their God was and the wonder of His rescuing them, He released the walls of water to fall upon the Egyptians. This is the part of the story most of us know, but I really want to focus on what the Israelites did next.

> *"When the people of Israel saw the mighty power that the Lord had unleashed against the Egyptians, they were filled with great awe before him. They put their faith in the Lord and in his servant Moses. Then Moses and the people of Israel sang [a] song to the Lord...Then Miriam the prophet, Aaron's sister, took a tambourine and led all the women as they played their tambourines and danced."*
> - *Exodus 14:31-15:1,20 (NLT)*

What did they do after seeing the Lord come to their rescue? They were filled with awe. They put their faith in the Lord. They praised. They sang and danced and rejoiced at the work of the Lord in their lives that very day. They didn't look at what happened and think, "That was pretty cool," and then continue on their way. They didn't immediately move on to the next part of their journey. They stopped where they were and praised the Lord for who He is and what He had just done for them. They took the time to celebrate the victory they had just witnessed and experienced. And after Moses and the people had praised, Miriam decided to lead the women in their own praise-song, again lifting up the power of their Deliverer. As

Erin Davis writes in a She Reads Truth Bible devotional, "Miriam paused and worshiped God for what He had delivered her from, before moving on to where she wanted Him to take her next." [8]

I hope you see the correlation between this story and yours. If you don't, let me ask you this: How did you do it? How did you overcome the pain? How did you know you needed to move, literally or figuratively? How did you land your job or your new position? Were there times when you wanted to give up because it seemed too difficult? Were there moments where everything seemed lost and there was no solution in sight? Did it take more than a few job interviews to land the job you're beginning now?

You may not have physically seen a sea split down the middle, providing an unmistakable path for you to make it to the other side, but I can almost guarantee you've had a "Red Sea moment."

A moment where the Lord made a way where there seemed like there wasn't one. A window that opened when all the doors were locked shut. A job interview or a new opportunity that "came out of nowhere." A college degree with your name on it after years of struggling both financially and academically. A trade school certificate that represents a way of providing for your family. An unexpected healing.

Think of your Red Sea moment, or any moment the Lord brings to mind that tells of His ability to provide or defend or rescue you, and praise Him for it. Think of the new job you are about to begin or have just begun. Think of the new step you have just taken. Whatever your new beginning is today, even if the beginning looks like a sunrise marking the start of a new day, stop for a moment and praise the Lord for it. Stopping to celebrate does not mean the hard parts are over, as we will soon see together, but it's a spectacular way of framing the present moment. So praise Him.

Praise Him as Miriam and the Israelites did at the Red Sea. Praise

His character, who He is by nature, and praise Him specifically for how He brought you here. Praise Him for the newness of it all. Don't jump immediately into the next thing. Celebrate where you are right now by the grace of God. Take time to look back at how far you've come and to appreciate the fingerprints of God in every season that led you to this one.

In my own life, I've recently started a new job. It's still in the realm of my college degree, but it is a much different take on the profession. I have moved from preparing tax returns in public accounting to working as a staff accountant in the financial accounting world. For those who aren't in the accounting profession, this means the rules I have to follow now are completely different than I've known and worked under for the past four years. It's a daunting task to change gears and think about the same numbers from a different perspective. It's tough and I'm definitely starting on a new learning curve, but God is here with me.

He has brilliantly opened the door for me to take the position I now have when I didn't even know the door was there to start with. He has provided financially in the transition period. He has revealed His providence, specifically in the last year of my life. He has allowed me to be a part of an organization that does so much good for the city of Nashville. He has given me new life and a fresh wave of energy to do the work He is calling me to do. And I praise Him for it. God has revealed Himself to be my Provider, my Sustainer, my Protector, and my Encourager. He has filled me with courage to step out and make a career move. He has given me joy and showed me grace in the overwhelming moments where I feel extremely unsure of my intelligence as I try to learn my new responsibilities. He has guided my heart back to Him after a season of striving. He is good, and I praise Him for these very things.

It's easy for me to want to rush ahead and say, "Okay, I'm here. I'm in this new job and I don't have everything down yet, but what's next? What's the next step for me, God?" But I'm learning to be present and celebrate the now. My hope is that you will learn with me that in order to appreciate the right now work of the Lord in our lives, we have to stop to look around us and "smell the roses." Please don't rush to get ahead in this moment.

Our time will come for greater responsibility and influence, but first, we must begin right where we are. Learning every day about our role, our community, our leaders, and ourselves. Growing by the day with each new opportunity we're given. Developing relationships with the people around us while maintaining the relationships we've developed in the past. Cultivating gratitude for being alive and able in the first place.

Have you ever read the parable of the three servants in Matthew 25? In this parable, we see three servants given bags of silver according to their abilities. These servants were called to be stewards, entrusted with their master's money. When the master returned, the two servants who used their ability to invest the money and grow its value were told *"Well done, my good and faithful servant. You have been faithful in handling this small amount, so now I will give you many more responsibilities. Let's celebrate together."*[9]

Y'all, this is what the Lord is telling us now. We have been faithful in handling the work He has given us, we have been obedient even it was hard and when the course seemed like a dead end. And now, as we embark on a new season of life or a new step in the journey, the Lord is saying, "Let's celebrate together." He demonstrates in this parable that when we are faithful in the small things, He will give us more responsibilities, but before He gives us those new responsibilities, He wants us to celebrate. He wants to celebrate with us.

These moments we're experiencing are exciting and difficult and scary all at the same time because the truth is, we don't really know what to do when we first hit unfamiliar ground. I'm being reminded of this fact every day as I walk into my new office and am asked questions to which I don't yet know the answer. And just like I'm asking you to do now, I'm trying so desperately to enjoy it and embrace it and celebrate it because it's a step forward, and every step forward deserves a celebration. As I celebrate this new season I'm walking into, I'm holding tight the words I felt the Lord whisper to my heart as I took my step forward:

"Now you're ready for what I have planned for you next. Today, your next step becomes your now step."

When your effort pays off in alignment with God's timing and God's plan, that is something to celebrate every single time. Embrace this moment of newness, of the Lord revealing the step you're now being asked to take. Even if you don't know what's next, celebrate what's now.

How do you celebrate the now when you still have to get up and go to work every day? When you aren't given time like the Israelites to literally stop moving and sing praise songs for a few days before continuing on your journey? Just because you're physically at work doesn't mean you can't celebrate the step you took to get there. When you're sitting at your new desk or in your new office, celebrate by doing your tasks with a grateful heart and a humble spirit. When you're walking down the halls or around town, celebrate by walking with joy and sharing that joy with a genuine smile and a "Hey, how's it going?" to the people you pass. When you're sitting in traffic in the morning, jam out to the latest praise song and turn your heart to the God Who shows up every day in your life. The list can go on and on because, really, celebrating doesn't mean we have to bring out the balloons and lift our hands to the sky (although you can totally do that). Celebrating means being present to enjoy what the Lord is doing in our "now step" and appreciating how He brought us here.

In his book, *The Pursuit of God*, A.W. Tozer wrote, "Let every man abide in the calling wherein he is called and his work will be as sacred as the work of the ministry. It is not what a man does that determines whether his work is sacred or secular, it is why he does it."[10] Our work, whether it takes place in a church or a school or an office, is of eternal value when we are walking with the Lord and stepping when He says to step. Being a part of such a sacred mission is praiseworthy because of the God behind the work. At the end of the day, the best expression of celebrating the work to which we are called is doing that work well, for the benefit of those around us and above all for the glory of God who filled us with purpose and ability to do this work. Now the question becomes: how do we work well?

AS YOU GROW UP: A LETTER FROM EMILY LAN

Take a moment and marvel at where you are and who you have become. Remember the grief that taught you empathy, the mistake that gave you wisdom, and the suffering that strengthened you, because despite of what has happened, you grew.

I remember a time when my definition of what is worthy of celebration was somewhat limited to accomplishments, an additional plaque on the wall or another step up the ladder, but over time, I've come to see just how narrow that view is. Genuine celebration that feeds the soul is not focused on what I've done. It's focused on what God has done for me, especially when I am at my weakest and facing the most impossible circumstances. Growing up is not easy, and there will be times when the road ahead seems impassable. In those times, you need to remember and celebrate the miracles God has already performed in your life.

Forty years after God parted the Red Sea, He parted the Jordan River so that Joshua could lead the people of Israel to the promise land. And He gave this command while the water was still held back, "Take twelve stones from the very place where the priests are standing in the middle of the Jordan. Carry them out and pile them up at the place where you will camp tonight." (Joshua 4:3 NLT) Why? Joshua explained, "In the future your children will ask, 'What do these stones mean?' Then you can tell them, 'This is where the Israelites crossed the Jordan on dry ground.' For the Lord your God dried up the river right before your eyes, and he kept it dry until you were all across, just as he did at the Red Sea when he dried it up until we had all crossed over. He did this so all the nations of the earth might know that the Lord's hand is powerful, and so you might fear the Lord your God forever." (Joshua 4:21-24 NLT)

Take a minute and dwell on an instance when you knew beyond a shadow of a doubt that God's hand was on your life, protecting and guiding you. Press that memory deep into your heart, maybe draw a symbol of it on a Post-It and stick it in your wallet and find a way to make yourself think of it often. We all need to gather our personal remembrance stones and pile them high because we have such a tendency to forget. When challenges big and small arise, look to your stones and remember that God is powerful and good, and He is good to you.

CHAPTER 3
Slow Your Role

Do you see those signs on the road sometimes that tell you there is a limit to how fast you can drive? Hopefully the answer to that question is "yes" if you've ever been behind the wheel of a car, but the real question is: do you follow the speed limit? Maybe you do, maybe you don't. I most definitely do...occasionally. One night as I was driving home at approximately ten miles over the speed limit, I felt this stirring in my heart. It wasn't a guilt-driven feeling about how fast I was driving, but it was a guilt-driven feeling about how fast I was *living*. The Lord just grabbed hold of my lead-foot that night and said, "Slow down. You are not racing to cross the finish line first." As much as the *Talledega Nights*-obsessed part of me wanted to shout, "If you ain't first, you're last," I had to admit that this was a message I needed to pay attention to. I think it's a message we all need to hear as we begin something new.

I don't know about you, but I have never wanted to waste time. I thought because I *can* do all of this so quickly that I *should* do all of this so quickly, because then I'll move on to the next thing in the shortest amount of time. I'll finish first. And so that's what I did. I finished school in three years, got my CPA license in less than a year, and started a job where I had my sights set on a promotion the day

I signed my offer letter. As God typically works, things went a bit sideways after about eight months on the job. I went from pushing and fighting and racing to finish first to not being able to do anything at all. I could barely work, I could barely get to work, and then I didn't work for more than two months. It was hard, and it definitely messed with my plan of being promoted faster than anyone else. But that time of forced slow down really did help me learn to slow down once I got back in the swing of things at work and in life in general...for a while...and then I started creeping back into my old familiar drive-too-fast, work-too-hard mindset. Then there I was, on the night the Lord reminded me as He always has that it's not about finishing first. It's about finishing well. It's about finishing faithfully. It's about finishing the job He has placed me on this earth at this time to do. And it's also about finishing that work in God's timeline, not my own.

In hindsight, nobody really cares how fast (or slow) you finish college. Most people don't remember who won the gold in the 100m freestyle swim at the Olympics, but they remember the athlete who battled cancer to come back and swim because that is what he was created to do and that is what he had trained to do. I'm not saying it's wrong to want to win. I want to win at literally anything I do, but it is crucial to remember what the most important "win" is. The SEC championship may be an important win, but if you win the championship game and forget who gave you the talent and ability to play the game, you've missed the point. The title of CEO or CFO might be the role you work towards all your career, but if you get that corner office and fancy title but turn your back on the people who helped you get there and the God who opened the doors that got you there, you've lost sight of everything that really matters.

One of my favorite passages in the Bible is 1 Corinthians 9:24-27 (NLT). In these verses, Paul relates being a follower of Christ to being an athlete. He says:

"Don't you realize that in a race everyone runs, but only one person gets the prize? So run to win! All athletes are disciplined in their training. They do it to win a prize that will fade away, but we do it for an eternal prize. So I run with purpose in every step. I am not just shadowboxing. I discipline my body like an athlete, training it to do what it should. Otherwise, I fear that after preaching to others I myself might be disqualified."

There is so much goodness and truth here that I don't know that I can adequately pick it apart, but there are three words I want to share which serve as guidelines for me in learning to navigate work and faith in order to finish well:

1. Purpose

2. Authenticity

3. Discipline

PURPOSE

Paul clearly knew what his purpose was, and he ran "with purpose in every step." He recognized he was called to share the Good News to anyone and everyone who could hear him. They may not listen, or they may listen and decide his messages were so radical he belonged in jail, but even this didn't stop him from sharing the Gospel of Christ because he knew this was the most important thing he could do with his life. He recognized the goal of the heaven-bound race was not to be the first one to cross the finish line but to bring as many people as possible across with him. He recognized the prize of winning this race was not a gold medal or a Stanley Cup, but an eternal inheritance and the joy and privilege and honor of being called a child of God.

I believe the Lord has given believers a sole purpose, but the expressions of that sole purpose are as unique as the faces you pass on the street and as numerous as the stars in the sky. Our primary purpose

is to share the Gospel and to go forth and make disciples.[11] If you
have chosen to follow Jesus, this is your purpose. For those who are
not called to the life of a full-time missionary, minister, or pastor,
this purpose is often expressed in our work. In her book, *Work, Love,
Pray,* Diane Paddison writes, "You probably will have no other
place where you have as much of an opportunity to influence others
toward God than in the workplace."[12]

In our workplace, we don't always get to decide who we work with.
I have worked with people of different religions, of no religion, of
different nationalities, and of different family backgrounds. For a
believer, this is an incredible opportunity to "make disciples of all
the nations"[13] because the nations can often be found in our office.
In living out our primary purpose in the workplace, we don't have
to shout the name of Jesus every day or wear a cross in some form of
jewelry to get the point across. We do have to "live a life worthy of
the gospel of Christ."[14] In our attitudes, our work ethic, our manner-
isms, and our words, we demonstrate our love for God and our love
for others.

AUTHENTICITY

"I am not just shadowboxing." Okay, I really love this part. In case
you don't know what this means, shadowboxing basically means
boxing against a "shadow" or an imaginary opponent. It's the kind
of training you do where you just throw punches at the air with no
real target to hit. I may have thrown punches at the air while doing
a boxing workout at home (because gyms are scary to me), but
fighting the air seems pointless after about thirty minutes. Fighting
opponents we don't truly see as real does, too.

Part of our race is that we are fighting against a real enemy. As
humans in this fallen world, we have struggles and our sinful nature
consistently tries to drag us down. When we forget our opponent—
our very own human nature—is throwing real punches including a

few we don't even realize until we're knocked off our feet, we need to remember that while we run the race toward heaven, our victory is already won. Sin has been defeated and through Christ, we are free to walk in the light!

When we remember our enemy and the victory we have in Christ, we are able to run our race with purpose and authenticity. If our purpose is spreading the Gospel, then we need to do that in every part of our lives. This means our faith is just as critical in the office as in the sanctuary. This also means as we live out our faith, we have to be real. As believers, we aren't made for the "fake it 'til you make it" lifestyle. Living out our faith is not a call to slap on a happy face even when our world is crashing down around us; it is a call to tell of the joy found in Christ even in the midst of grief or pain. It's a call to show love to every person who crosses our path through our willingness to hear them out and relate to them as a human being made in the image of the same Creator and full of every ounce of dignity and worth we have ourselves.

If we're struggling with anxiety, we let people into our struggle and maybe even use that as an opportunity to tell of God's unshakable nature. If we're on a mountaintop, we rejoice and tell of the goodness of the God Who put us on that mountain. If we didn't get enough sleep the night before and need a triple shot of espresso in our coffee, we warn our coworkers and then ask for forgiveness if we get a little snappy before the coffee kicks in. If we need help, we ask for it. We serve people, we love people, we do the work we're asked to do, and then we do a little more.

DISCIPLINE

Paul recognized the importance of being disciplined so much he mentions it twice. He mentions it in setting up the example of how an athlete is disciplined in their training and again in explaining that he disciplines his body "like an athlete, training it to do what it should."

I was once given the opportunity to hear Joan Cronan, former women's athletic director at the University of Tennessee in Knoxville during the Pat Summit-era, speak at a conference. She shared a story of Pat Summit asking girls attending youth basketball camps if they had made their bed every morning. It seems like such a weird question because what does making your bed have to do with basketball? But Pat Summit knew the value of discipline, and while I never had the privilege of meeting her during this life, I think she knew the art of discipline permeated every aspect of our lives. I think Paul knew the same thing. He knew what his purpose was and he trained endlessly to accomplish that purpose. As with Paul and Pat Summit, our discipline comes in two forms: faith and fact.

You may have been called to ministry in a church setting or called to live out your faith in some other vocation, but either way, if you have given your life to Christ and been raised to new life through His sacrifice, your primary purpose is to bring Him glory in this world. Your vocation is secondary, but both purposes require discipline.

In my own life, I know that, to do my job well, I need to be connected to God and also competent to do the task I've been assigned. The foundation of my discipline is that I need to be in the word of God every day. I need to be disciplined in seeking God each and every day. I need to be disciplined in maturing through every season of life as I see and experience more of who He is and what He is doing in my life and in the world around me. I also need to work on my competence in my professional field. I need to take the continuing professional education courses to stay up-to-date on the industry standards. I need to grow in my knowledge of how to present myself professionally in business meetings and communications.

I'm drawn to the example of Luke in this area of discipline. In Acts 20:24 (NLT) Luke says, *"But my life is worth nothing to me unless I use it for finishing the work assigned me by the Lord Jesus—the work of telling others the Good News about the wonderful grace of God."* Luke gets it. He knew his work on this earth was to tell of the Good News, but guess what? Luke was a doctor. He had a vocation apart from his sharing of the Gospel, and I think that fact makes his words sweeter. He, like many of us today, had a call to not only share the Gospel but also had a job outside of the church, and he learned to do both well.

I don't know what it took to be a doctor during Luke's time, but I imagine there to be extensive training in the form of an apprenticeship. Let's think about what it takes to be a doctor today. Four years of undergraduate schooling, four years of medical school beyond that, and then three or more years as a medical intern or resident before the final boards to officially be called an MD. Talk about needing discipline. I'm no doctor, but I don't think you can slack your way through all of that. Not only do you need discipline to study during school and train on-the-job during residency, you need discipline to just not give up.[15] You need discipline to stay on track, to push through the long nights and bad patient outcomes. And once you start practicing as a doctor on your own, you must stay disciplined to do your job well, to care for your patients, and stay updated on medical advancements.

So in our work, whatever it may be, we must remember the intertwined purpose of both our work and our faith and run the race laid out for us personally. Don't get caught up in trying to beat someone out of a job or a promotion. Don't get tripped up by jealousy when someone climbs the corporate ladder faster. Don't try to "fake it 'til you make it." Be real with where you are and be disciplined in staying connected to God first and doing your job well. Remember that while winning is a good thing, we don't win the true race by cutting corners and bashing the reputation of another. We may get ahead in our career if we try to win this way, but in the end, we might find ourselves in the position Paul feared: disqualified from the race that ends in eternity with God. Life gets hard and challenges will no doubt come our way, but at the end of our lives, when we've retired from our professional work and accomplished our spiritual job on this earth, I hope we can all look back and honestly share the words of 2 Timothy 4:7-8 (NLT):

> *"I have fought the good fight, I have finished the race, and I have remained faithful. And now the prize awaits me - the crown of righteousness, which the Lord, the righteous Judge, will give me on the day of his return..."*

Our race has already begun and in order to finish well, we must fight the good fight. We must remember our purpose, run with that purpose honestly and authentically, and be consistent in our discipline. These words are easy to type but so difficult to live out. In the next few chapters, I want to invite you into the struggles I've faced and the battles I continue to fight. I hope that in telling these stories and the words of God that have helped me walk through struggles, you will recognize you are not alone in yours. You are not alone period. We are in this fight together, for the good of others and the glory of God.

AS YOU GROW UP: A LETTER FROM SHEA DAVIS

I remember when I learned my first real life / business lesson: adding value. I was an investment banker in NYC and had been working ninety plus hour weeks. When I was recruited, my future boss told me that if I worked as hard and as smart as he expected, I could easily be an early promotee in a year. At my first review my boss praised my hard work and gave accolades for all I had accomplished and my salary raise was 10.8302849%. Well, now isn't that an odd number? I had a friend in finance and asked what the average raise was for my level at the firm that year. How could my raise be the exact average if my boss said I was exceptional? I went to his office and asked this with as much couth as I could muster and his response was simple: "You work hard and you did good work, but it is nothing I can't hire someone else to do or do myself. Right now you are learning on my nickel and I am investing in you. I just hope one day you pay dividends…" I thanked him and excused myself to go be more humble.

What I wish I'd known then is the importance of being generous. Most folks think being generous means giving extra money to a charity or church, or to the homeless person on the street. I view generosity in the strictest of definitions: showing a readiness to give more of something than is strictly necessary or expected. When someone needs your patience, kindness, help or comfort, the ability to be generous is as Christ-like as I can think to be. This ranges in all parts of life, from personal to professional. When a person you would never be interested in asks you out, you can be generous in your response. If you offend, apologize with generosity and sincerity. While attending a work function and you see someone alone and uncomfortable, you have an amazing opportunity to be generous and welcoming. By focusing on generosity, you can show the world how Jesus works through you and make others feel comforted.

So I pray you would remember as you're Growing Up that God gave you talents and He revels in your success. Not everything will be easy because you are a Christian, in fact, sometimes it may be harder. You will not always make the best decisions and learning from those is what He wants for you. Seek reflection, seek counsel of others and pray for strength. There are so many great quotes and mantras out there and I encourage you to seek those that will affect you. On my mirror I have "Don't be Afraid to Fail, Be Afraid Not to Try." My personal mantra is "Pain is Temporary, Glory is Forever" and it got me through three marathons. Find yours...

CHAPTER 4
Forget the Coin Toss

Recently, I read a book written by a pastor with more than thirty years of ministry experience. The book was incredible, but reading the words of the extremely knowledgeable and faithful pastor and then thinking of my desire to write this very book gave way to a lot of doubt. My hope for this book is you can see the authenticity I am trying so hard to write with. I want this book to be honest and relatable, but with that desire comes the reality that I am not and may never be as knowledgeable as the writer of that book.

The words in this book may not be structured as clearly or eloquently, but that doesn't mean my words aren't just as real. I don't at this point have as much experience or biblical training, but that's why I want to write this book now. I am a single, young professional, who is stepping into a new career path. I'm not thirty plus years into my career, I'm three years in. (While I'm at it, let me just tell you I have had zero training on how to write a book beyond the required English courses for any non-English college degree, a few podcasts, and most recently, a support system called Hope*Writers.)

The doubts that I can actually do this come flooding in when I read books by well-established authors and teachers. The ability to create something from scratch, to mold together enough ideas to bind them

up and sell them to the public is incredibly powerful and unique. I
am so thankful for the authors who have written the books I've read
over the years...but I never really thought I would join their ranks.

Maybe I won't. Maybe I'll just write all this down and put it together
and keep it to myself. Maybe I will have the privilege of publishing
this and no one will read it. Maybe my family and friends will be
the only ones who ever see or buy it. Maybe people will buy it but
not like it or even hate it. These are the thoughts that fill my mind as
I read other books and think about how they are better than mine
may possibly be. These thoughts even fill my mind now, not as I read
something else, but as I pour my deepest, most insecure thoughts
onto paper in the middle of a crowded coffee shop.

I let these thoughts simmer in my mind too often, but I also think
about God, who says that I am created with purpose. I am created
with desires and gifts and a uniqueness He can use for His glory if
only I give up mine. He reminds me that, when molding my heart,
He filled it with a desire to come alongside and encourage women,
and when molding my mind, He filled it with enough words and
thoughts to fill a book. Then He reminds me that as He molded
all of me together, He made the two—heart and mind—to work
together. And just as He did then, He is now taking the thoughts in
my mind, matching them up with the desires of my heart, and giving
me a story to tell and an opportunity to share.

The Lord reminds me that even though I don't feel qualified to write
these words, and even if I'm legitimately not qualified to write these
words, He doesn't need me to be qualified before obeying His call.
That's kind of His thing. He calls us and if we are willing to answer,
He makes us qualified. He gives us the literal or metaphorical words
to write a book.

He may not give me all the words at once, but He will faithfully give
me one word at a time, one thought at a time, one chapter at a time,

until I've written all He has called me to write. In some situations, He may give us everything we need in the blink of an eye, as He has for so many believers spreading the Gospel. The similar monster of doubt whispers in their ear, "You won't know what to say. You won't be able to answer the questions they throw at you. You won't change anything." But when the obedient answer the call of the Lord to share the Gospel, He shows up right then and there. He reminds us He knows what to say, He can answer any questions, and He changes everything. He reminds us that, in our obedience, He fills us with His wisdom and knowledge so we can join Him in accomplishing His purposes.

In the midst of one of my self-doubt montages, a friend sent me the following quote, and it has spoken to my heart time and time again. I've even taped it to my laptop so I have to read it every time I write. My initial thought was, "Great. Another author who is better at writing than me." Then the Lord calmed my heart, silenced the doubt, and asked me to read it one more time. After reading it a second time, my heart was bubbling over at how the author seemed to read my mind and answer my doubting questions.

> *"Too many authors worry about whether or not their book will get published. That isn't the question. The question is this: Are you called to write? That's the only question you need to answer. And if the answer is yes, then you need to write the book as an act of obedience. It doesn't matter whether anyone reads it or not."[16]*

You may not be writing a book. You might be starting your first full-time position in your chosen field, shifting your career path, or starting over completely. Whatever your situation, read this quote again but replace the words with your situation. "Too many nurses worry about whether or not they can heal their patient…" "Too many college graduates worry about whether or not they will be good at their job…" "Too many entrepreneurs worry about whether or not they will be successful with their new small business..."

I don't know about you, but this quote not only gives me courage to keep going, it gives me enthusiasm to write to the best of my abilities because I do feel called to write. So I'm doing this thing. I'm writing and I'm typing and I'm pouring out my heart because my heart has been filled to the brim by its Creator and the only fitting response is for me to pour out the good and watch as He fills it once again.

This is what each of these chapters represent. With every chapter, the Lord has worked in my heart as He has worked through my life. These are the lessons I've learned, the experiences that taught me the lessons, the life within the experiences, and the God who orchestrated it all. I'm blessed to have lived the life I have to this point, and I cannot credit that life to anyone or anything but the good Lord who created me and whose image I bear. I am no queen (and really, I think I'd rather just settle for being a duchess), but in writing these words I find myself asking much the same thing Mordecai asked Esther as she began to recognize the Lord's call on her life, "Who knows if perhaps you were made queen for just such a time as this?"[17]

When I sit back and remember these things (the call of the Lord, the obedience of my answer, and the faithfulness of the Lord to be with me every step of the way), I see things more clearly. I see this is something I am called to do. I see the way the Lord is shifting my own heart even now as new pieces start to fit together. Most recently, I see that the doubts I have stem from comparing myself to others.

I think most of the self-doubt we struggle with stems from the way we compare ourselves with others, and that comparison can quickly take a turn towards envy. We look at the beauty queen and think, "I could never look like her." The beauty queen looks at another beauty queen and thinks much the same thing. We look at the CEO of our company and think, "I'm not that smart and doubt I ever will be, so why bother with trying?" The CEO looks at the CEO of a larger company and thinks, "Yeah my company is doing well. We're profitable, we've got a great company culture and dedicated employees, and we've built relationships with our customers and community... but THAT CEO just announced a huge merger which will double his annual income. Why can't I be like him or her?" We look at our neighbor to the right and think, "They've got the coolest car or the nicest yard or the cutest children." Meanwhile our neighbor to the left looks at us and thinks "They always look happy and they act like they truly enjoy each others company. That's the life I want."

We have all compared ourselves to someone else, so it's no surprise we ultimately can end up with feelings of jealousy towards that person, but how do we feel when we compare ourselves to someone else and think we're better off? Well y'all, this would be my old friend: pride.

When I first started thinking of this comparison struggle, I knew I wanted to talk about pride because I have lived it, capital L- Lived it. I talked before about my current struggle of comparison revealing itself as being jealous of writers I see as "better" than me. But I've also found myself on the other side of the comparison fence.

Growing up, I was always the "goodie-good." The girl who never broke the rules, never snuck out of the house to go to the party down in someone's field, never got a B in school (until English Literature in college). I grew up being the daughter of parents who were well-known in the community, so I thought I had to be this girl—we'll get into the image implications of that problem later. My mom used to tell us before we left the house: "Remember, I have spies everywhere!" And let me just say she honestly did, not because she paid people to follow us everywhere but because people just knew who I was and to whom I belonged. So goes the life of a small-town gal whose mother is a high school teacher and father is a business owner.

I don't want you to think I'm mad about the way I grew up. I loved my childhood and my parents and my town and I wouldn't trade those things for all the money in the world. But growing up as the "goodie-good" translated to me believing I was "better" than the people who went out drinking on the weekends or who didn't make the honor roll in school or who weren't sitting in a church pew on Sunday morning. This thought process in no way was pushed or encouraged by my parents; it was me. It was my misguided belief that, because I was doing things the "right" way, God was more pleased with me than with the other girl or guy who messed up more visibly. Sadly, this thought process kept rolling through high school... through college...and right through the doors of the office.

I would complete a tax return faster than another person, so I was better. I wouldn't have as many corrections on a return than the person who prepared it the year before, so I was better. This thought process is so destructive, and honestly it's something I haven't been able to kick to the curb overnight. Just like feeling jealous of someone who has more or does better work than I do, casting my pride out the door is a process. It's a struggle I fight over and over again. Both sides of the comparison coin are tough, but our God is so much tougher.

In the battle of comparison, we have to remember the words of our Savior. We have to know the truth and be able to shut down the lies of the enemy that tell us we need to do more to be accepted, we need to have more to be liked, and we need to be more to be loved. On the flip side of the comparison coin, we also need to know the truth to silence the voices that say we don't need to do more because we're already better than the other person, we're liked more than the next person because we have more, and we are loved because we are the good girl.

Ephesians 1:4-8 (NLT) says this:

> *"Even before he made the world, God loved us and chose us in Christ to*

be holy and without fault in his eyes. God decided in advance to adopt us into his own family by bringing us to himself through Jesus Christ. This is what he wanted to do, and it gave him great pleasure. So we praise God for the glorious grace he has poured out on us who belong to his dear Son. He is so rich in kindness and grace that he purchased our freedom with the blood of his Son and forgave our sins. He has showered his kindness on us, along with all wisdom and understanding."

Loved, chosen, adopted, freed, forgiven. This is who we are. This is a gift from God, who made us worthy of such kindness through the sacrifice of his Son.

Why do we work for acceptance when we are offered this great gift? We don't have to work to earn these things because He chose to offer them to us before the world was made. We don't have to compare ourselves with other people because we have already been accepted by God and would rather spend our time praising God for the glorious grace He has poured out on us.

Why do we believe we are better off than the next person when God decided these things in advance? Just as God chose to offer us these things before we messed up, He also chose to offer us these things before we did things right. And even more so, we can't hold onto the pride in our hearts because we needed to be freed from and forgiven for our sins just as much as the person to which we compared ourselves.

Y'all, these words are life-giving and life-changing. They bring me joy as I look at the kindness God has showered on me. They renew my mindset as it shifts from working to be better than the next person to living and working from the knowledge of who God says I am and who He has made me to be. They bring me courage to chase the seeming impossible or even ludicrous (like writing a book when I'm not a "writer") as I experience what Louie Giglio described as living from acceptance, not for it.[18]

I don't know about you, but I definitely don't find courage in self-doubt and comparison. I find fear which cripples me to the point I cannot move forward. I find myself leaning on pride as I look for ways I am better than someone else to somehow reassure myself I am worthy of doing what I'm trying to do. The word "self-doubt" itself points to the wrong person. If I had to rely on myself then the doubts are definitely valid. As I lean instead on the words of Truth, I'm reminded these things are not from the Father. Proverbs 27:4 calls jealousy "even more dangerous" than anger, and 1 John 2:16 calls pride in our achievements "from this world."

Paul knew this struggle was real and present in many areas of the world, even in his time. He cautioned the believers in Rome, "Don't think you are better than you really are...In his grace, God has given us different gifts for doing certain things well."[19] And later to the church in Galatia he says, "Pay careful attention to your own work, for then you will get the satisfaction of a job well done, and you won't need to compare yourself to anyone else."[20]

When we live in the truths that we are chosen, accepted, loved, and worthy, all gifted by the blood of Christ, we begin to accept ourselves, love ourselves, and find a reprieve from comparison because we are children of God. It is then and only then that we find the joy that Bob Goff summed up in saying "We won't be distracted by comparison if we are captivated by purpose."[21]

Comparison is not a new struggle. It was present in the days of Paul and it is present in our lives today, but as we recognize our acceptance by the blood of Christ, we find the purpose which keeps us working and living out our faith well. We find freedom in the truth of 2 Corinthians 3:5 (NLT) which says, "It is not that we think we are qualified to do anything on our own. Our qualification comes from God." We find we are able to work by the grace of God and power of His Spirit within us. We are able to take the step into a new, unfamiliar space as we trust the God who is calling us to step. We aren't hindered by people outperforming us and we aren't boastful when we finish our work first. We are working from the knowledge we are called by God to be where we are and do what we're doing. That, my friends, is much more worthwhile than comparison, don't you think?

AS YOU GROW UP: A LETTER FROM BRIANNA MORTON

There are a few times in my life I remember so well the same emotions I experienced in those very life changing moments are evoked. There are people, words, and thoughts I recall as if they happened yesterday. Moments of sadness, anxiety, grief, adversity, and most importantly, growth.

I want to tell you about two very specific times in my life which shook me to my core. Moments I will never forget for the rest of my life. Moments I share with others, in hopes of inspiring them to press on and believe in a greater future. The first was the night before my first day of college. I remember crying uncontrollably and asking my mother if I had to start college. I remember thinking I couldn't go, that I wasn't smart enough, I wouldn't make friends, teachers wouldn't like me, and I couldn't be anything more than I was at that moment: a scared kid who was expected to be an adult now and lacked the confidence. My mother consoled me for hours. She reminded me of Joshua 1:9: "Be strong and courageous, do not be frightened or dismayed for the Lord your God is with you wherever you go." She promised to help me get to my first class. She and I got ready the morning of my first day. She drove in her car and I drove mine. We arrived in the parking lot of the University of North Alabama shortly after 7 am. I cried with my mother and we prayed for me to have the strength to get through the first class. Around 7:40, my mother had calmed me enough to walk to my first class. Filled with nervousness, I entered the building and walked up the stairs only to see four of my former classmates waiting for the same class. Flash forward, I spent the rest of the day nervous, and honestly the next five years I was somewhat nervous, but after "surviving" the first day, I knew college was something I had to complete.

The second moment was oddly a little less scary because of the first: the day I told my mother I was pregnant. I also expressed I didn't feel like I could continue the job I had at the time. I had also recently moved away from my family. I had to find a way to make many things work in a new town without a job and wondering if I could be the best mom my soon-to-be daughter deserved. I remember telling my mother with such sadness, because I loved the work I was doing, and with calmness, because my mother had been the best example for being an exceptional parent. I remember praying I would be able to take care of this precious gift and that I possessed the tools to provide and care for the person who would become the most important person in my life. I believe a verse that is a great representation of what we need to remember is Deuteronomy 31:6, 8: "Be strong and bold; have no fear or dread of them, because it is the Lord your God who goes before you. He will be with you; he will not fail you or forsake you."

I pray you would remember this as you're Growing Up: The Lord never puts more on us than we can bear with His help. You aren't better than anyone else and no one else is better than you. We are given strength we don't know we have and if we lead a life of service, hold on to hope, and have faith there is a greater life promised beyond this earthly world, we will find peace, purpose, and persistence toward our future.

CHAPTER 5
Fear Falling

As I write these words, my heart and my mind have been filled with fear. I know the Bible tells me "don't be afraid" many times, but sometimes those three words aren't enough to ease my fears. Sometimes when I'm sharing what scares me, I just want to scream at the person who simply says, "don't be afraid" or its worry counterpart, "don't worry." I need to know why. Why should I not be afraid? Why shouldn't I worry about this?

Right now, I'm in the midst of writing week after week, processing my innermost thoughts and hurts and hopes. Sharing the work of the Lord in my life, sharing my testimony. I'm writing these heart letters and these moments all in the possibility of one day publishing them (or most of them) for the world to see and read and judge and criticize. And that scares me.

Yesterday I allowed a doctor to stick seventy-one needles in my back to determine the truth about what I'm allergic to. Of those seventy-one needles, seven were specifically the source of my fear. They were foods I had gone twenty-four years believing I was allergic to but never really knowing the truth. Could they kill me if I ate them? Possibly. Could I be totally fine if I ate them? Possibly. But for twenty-four years, the first question won out and yesterday was the first time I was to know the truth. And that scared me.

At work I have been leading a project that would transform one of our finance processes. Researching companies, reading the proposal, fielding questions and concerns from upper management and executives, and (almost) having management on board to actually implement the process. With their approval, we will begin to implement the new system which will affect every department. All managers across the board will need to know how to use the system and understand what their responsibilities are, and that process will no doubt be a great undertaking. I will soon be part of a team of relatively new employees, telling managers who have been there for many years that they need to change their process and jump on board with the new system. And that situation scares me.

Over the past few months, the idea of me co-leading the Nashville chapter of 4word, a global nonprofit organization, has been floating around. I've been asked to step up with one of my close friends to lead the local women of Nashville to reach their God-given potential in their workplaces. As much as the thought of co-leading these women excites me, this shift involves taking the reins of an organization in which many of the members are older and wiser and more "suitable" for this role than I think I am. And that situation really scares me.

In the past week, I've been asked to be a part of a story spotlight at a women's event at my church. This would mean me sharing my testimony and the darkest parts of my story with women of all ages. This would mean me standing alongside a few other women also sharing their story, and I hear the old familiar inner-critic shouting at me that their stories are better, more "Jesus-y", and that they will be able to speak more clearly and concisely and everyone will like their stories better. And while I know that comparison shouldn't be a part of my story, this situation scares me too.

I think it's safe to say my mind is a bit jumbled at the moment, bringing me back to the age old battle of faith vs. fear, know vs. feel.

Ironically (and I promise you this was not at all planned), the shirt I'm wearing as I type this literally says, "faith / fear," which is meant to represent faith over fear. It's moments like these, the little ironies of life, that I believe God uses to remind me of truth, His Truth. The value of trusting in His Truth and walking by the faith I know deep in my soul, rather than giving in to the feeling of fear battling in my mind. In reminding me of Truth, I'm reminded that I desperately need the truth. I need to know the truth and write it on my heart for moments just like these.[22]

One of my favorite chapters in the entire Bible is Psalm 23. It's a chapter I have turned back to time and time again when I needed to be reminded of what life looks like when I let the Lord lead. This is the Psalm my heart reaches for when I'm in the grip of fear, when I feel like I've made a wrong turn, or when I can't *feel* His presence.

One February a few years ago, I was feeling this loss of God's presence in my life. I knew He was there. I knew He hadn't abandoned me. Yet it seemed like no matter how hard I tried, I couldn't feel His presence. I believe this also causes us to fear. We lose the "feeling" of God and we panic. Has He finally decided to give up on me? Have I really messed up this time and He's just done? Did I do something wrong or choose something that wasn't supposed to be mine and I won't be back in His good graces until I fix it? These are the fear-filled thoughts my mind goes to when I'm in what most people call the "desert place." Even when I know the truth, I sometimes let my feelings speak louder.

So that February, I turned once again to Psalm 23 and read it twice a day for the whole month, first thing in the morning and last thing at night. Y'all, when you can't *feel* God's presence in your life, *know* that His presence can be found in the words of Scripture. I didn't feel His presence rain down in my desert place immediately. He definitely could have made this happen, but this time He didn't and I think it was because He knew that I needed to write these words on my heart. So, every morning and every night for twenty-eight days I read these words:

> *The Lord is my shepherd, I have all that I need.*
> *He lets me rest in green meadows;*
> *He leads me beside peaceful streams.*
> *He renews my strength.*
> *He guides me along right paths, bringing honor to His name.*
> *Even when I walk through the darkest valley,*
> *I will not be afraid for you are close beside me.*
> *Your rod and your staff protect and comfort me*
> *You prepare a table for me in the presence of my enemies.*
> *You honor me by anointing my head with oil.*
> *My cup overflows with blessings.*
> *Surely goodness and unfailing love will pursue me all the days of my life,*
> *And I will dwell in the house of the Lord forever.*[23]

Even when we don't feel it, we can know this to be true. This is the "why." Verse four is one of those instances where we are told not to fear, but the words after it answer the question I want to shout out when I'm told to simply not be afraid "...*for you are close beside me...*"

When He is my Shepherd, when I let the Lord lead, I do not have to be afraid because He provides for my every need. He leads me to peace. He renews (or restores) my strength. He guides me down the path of righteousness. He is close beside me, even in the desert. He protects and comforts me. He prepares a table for me, a place for me to sit with Him, not after my enemies are defeated and not when all my fears are put to death, but in their midst. He fills my life with so many blessings I cannot keep them to myself. His goodness and unfailing love pursue me. I do not have to be afraid because I will dwell in the house of the Lord forever.

As I felt all of these fears welling up within me again, I began to open my Bible to this exact Psalm. Throughout the years my Bible has collected many notes that I wrote on little slips of paper (or napkins if that's all I could find), and as I attempted to open to the page of Psalm 23, I flipped instead to Psalm 37 because I just so happened to have a little note stuck in this page. Do you want to guess which two Psalms were included on this note? Psalm 37 because that's what page it was stuck to... and Psalm 23.

You might be thinking, "Big deal, you probably just wrote a note about Psalm 23 and then later needed a piece of paper for Psalm 37 and that note was the closest thing you had." And if you're thinking this, you are absolutely right. That's exactly what happened, but as I've walked with the Lord for a decade now, I've learned that even the smallest coincidences can be divinely intentional.

Psalm 37 is another one of my favorites, and for months I had verse seven as the background of my phone because I was in a season of wanting to go and go and go but I knew the Lord was calling me to wait and I needed the reminder Every. Single. Day. But today, as I flipped to the "wrong" chapter (I add quotation marks because really no chapter in the Bible is wrong, I just wanted to be dramatic about how my plan to read Psalm 23 was derailed), this verse seemed to jump out:

"Put your hope in the Lord. Travel steadily along his path."[24]

Then I flipped to Psalm 23, because that is originally what I wanted to read, and I was struck by verse three:

"He renews my strength. He guides me along right paths, bringing honor to his name."[25]

In both verses, I notice the mention of a path; more specifically *His* path, the *right* path. While these verses may not directly tell us "do not fear," I find myself fearing all the things I've mentioned above a little bit less. These verses remind me the path I am on is God's.

Doesn't it seem that in the times we are most afraid, we feel the weakest? It's like the act of being afraid just zaps us of any energy or strength we have in us to fight the fear. Our minds go into overdrive thinking of all the bad scenarios and we're left exhausted and feeling like a weakling who can't even muster the courage to face the fear, let alone fight it.

In all my fears, this is the theme. I feel like I am not strong enough to accomplish what's in front of me. I'm not good enough or old enough or smart enough or wise enough to see them through as they ought to be seen through. But that is the fear talking.

God calls us to put our hope in Him as we travel along His path, the path He has laid out for us and the opportunities He has provided to us. Not only do we travel along His path, but we travel steadily. We walk steadily into the places to which He leads us. We walk confidently into the space to which He is guiding us. The fears can trip us up and cause us to stumble along the path, but when He is leading us, when we fully release the reins into His capable hands, we can travel steadily. I don't know about y'all, but for a girl whose middle name is ironically "Grace," this brings peace. When I fear stumbling through life or even stumbling on a flat sidewalk on my way to work, God reminds me to put my hope in Him and be steadied, my feet and my heart.

He also reminds us that He renews our strength when we don't feel strong enough to share our story, or lead a group of women, or take the lead on a big project at work. He reminds us that He guides us along right paths when we fear taking on a responsibility not meant for us, when we fear saying "yes" is a misstep that will place us outside of His best for us.

Through all of this, He reminds us the key is connection with Him.

If we stay connected to God and His truth, if we seek His wisdom in making decisions and choosing when to say "yes" and when to say "no," if we write His words on our heart and remember our hope and our strength are not in ourselves but in a God who does not fail, then faith will overpower fear every day of the week. He will guide us along the right path as we walk by faith, and He will use our walk, our story, our job, our "yes" and our "no" to bring honor to His name.

I think now is a good moment to point out that I am not enough. I, in my own right, am not wise enough or brave enough to write a book or lead a group of women to Christ. If I didn't have Jesus, my fear is one-hundred percent valid, but when I lean into the Holy Spirit, when I rely on the wisdom and courage of the God I am writing and speaking for, He makes me enough. He fills these words. He opens my heart and my mind and my eyes to see what He is doing around me and He gives me a spark of courage to write it all down and share it with anyone willing to listen (thanks for hanging with me, friend).

It's when I take the step of obedience in faith, relying on His working in and through and from all of these words, I recognize He is equipping me as I go. If you've been a part of the church long enough, you've heard the words in some form or fashion that when God gives you an assignment for His kingdom, He equips you to do just that. And He does. He truly and whole-heartedly does. But we must step in obedience. We must accept the assignment, whether we see the equipping or not. We are not stepping haphazardly, hoping God will keep us steady. We are stepping with purpose and with intentionality born of the call of the Lord. We don't feel ready, but God is telling us to step so we step. We feel scared of where our feet might land as we pick one foot off the ground beneath us and stretch forward, but we pick our feet up and step because we know God is leading our stepping.

I am all about a good analogy, so in thinking about this idea of the Lord equipping us even in the midst of our fears, I start to think about my job. I currently work for an NHL team, and goodness there is a lot of equipment required to play a hockey game. Piece by piece, the guys start putting on the equipment, preparing their bodies and their minds for the upcoming competition. It's not like they pop in the locker room, snap their fingers, and then pop back out and onto the ice. It's a process, but by the time they get to the ice, by game-time, they are fully equipped and ready to play.

The same is true for the work to which God is calling us. When we first get the call, we step into the locker room. We start preparing ourselves and allowing God to prepare our hearts and minds for what's about to happen. Our obedience is stepping into the locker room, and God rejoices in that step. When God has fully equipped us, when it's game time and we've got to move again, we step out on the ice. Step up to the plate. Step onto the field. Use whatever sports metaphor you want, but we take the step in obedience and by faith knowing that, despite the nerves and the fear of failing, we are prepared and we have been equipped to do what we're about to do.

Last but certainly not least, I want to caution you against seeing your obedience as "small." No form of obedience to God is small. Whether we are being obedient in moving around the world or taking one step forward in faith as we choose what job we will take, or whispering, "Thy will be done," on what seems like the most difficult day of our lives, or handing out one dollar to the person on the street corner, no manner of obedience seems small or insignificant to God. He sees our battle as we intentionally choose to follow Him. He sees the fear or anxious thoughts as we push them aside, refusing to let them keep us from trusting His plan and His work for our lives. Our Shepherd sees us, He sees our obedience, and while our step may seem "small" to us, He rejoices in it.

Maybe you have recently stepped towards something new and that's why you're reading this book. Maybe you are standing at the end of what you know and are afraid to step into what is unknown. Fear will come in both places and thankfully, so will faith. Whether you are in the office or at the altar or anywhere in between, I hope you will remember fear will fall to faith when faith is rooted in the God Who is close beside you. I hope you will choose trust in God. I hope you will choose obedience.

AS YOU GROW UP: A LETTER FROM PAT ASP

I spent the first twenty-five years of my professional career afraid of being good enough, being dressed right, making the best Christian decision…the list goes on. You name it, I'd have a corresponding fear. Then having made the decision to retire rather than continue to work in an unacceptable situation (scared silly and the first of three retirements), my husband was diagnosed with cancer. Talk about a new level of fear. I was brought to my knees. Each instance of fearful events (and there were many), there I was on my knees.

UNTIL I realized that if I could see around the future corners of my life, there will always be times of great fear and times of great elation. The important "ah-ha" moment was to stay in continuous conversation with Him and to surrender all aspects of my life to Him, not only in times of fear, but all day and every day. I need to always be inviting Him in to my heart, mind and spirit, to be walking on His path and continually asking for discernment in choosing what His will is for my life. This continual conversation brings great peace, allowing me to face daily what He has in store for me and all those I love and hold close to my heart.

CHAPTER 6
Tell Me About Yourself

"Tell me about yourself."

Anyone who has sat in a job interview has probably heard this. It's the professional version of the question, "Who are you?"

If you're anything like me, you really, really, really hate this question. Every time I am asked this question, it's almost like I experience a minor identity crisis all over again. Even though I know the answer. I know that because I believe in Christ I am a child of God and a co-heir with Christ. I know that I am loved. I am saved. I am accepted. [26]

I could go on and on about who God says I am, and I would be happy to do so because we're told our identity is in Christ. Our Rock, our Redeemer, the One who took our sins and gave us the privilege of being identified as children of God. Our identity is in God, Who created us in His image, chose us for a specific purpose before we were even born, and still calls us personally by name out of His marvelous grace.

My identity in Christ is not under question. I know this to be true because I have experienced the life-changing grace and salvation that is found only in Christ. When we're told that our identity is in Christ, we're also told that our identity is not our job, our college degree, our extra curricular activities, our marital status, our ethnicity, our financial background, our family, or anything else. Only Christ.

Honestly, this is not the answer most people want to hear. Your interviewer does not want to be taken to church when the interview is for a corporate position. The guy you just met for a first date doesn't want to hear about how Jesus is the only man you *need* in your life (even though that is true). So how do you answer the question of who you are?

This is my struggle, and maybe it's yours, too. I know my identity is found in Christ and that identity ultimately dictates who I am and what I do. The question isn't where is my identity found. The question is what does finding my identity in Christ mean in the business world? How do I explain who I am without throwing out the name of Jesus in every sentence?

In questioning and praying and searching for a way to tell people in the workplace about myself without making everyone around me uncomfortable and only saying, "I'm a child of God," here's what I'm learning: my identity is in Christ, but that identity is expressed in many titles.

My worth, value, and salvation are firmly in Christ alone, and the things I do and the people I'm in a relationship with and the passion projects in my heart are part of what makes me, me. I am first and foremost a follower of Christ and a child of God, and I am also a CPA, a sister, a daughter, a friend, a single lady waiting on the man God stamps as "Courtney's future husband," a hockey fan, a writer, a member of the church, a young professional, a bookworm (especially during the colder months of the year), a brain surgery survivor, a lover of white chocolate mochas with an extra shot of espresso and no whipped cream, a hard worker, and a born and raised small-town Tennessean. All of these things are me. They make up who I am. For better or worse, these are all parts of the same me.

I think this a tricky topic because when we start identifying ourselves with certain labels it's easy to let those labels slip into the position of Christ. We talk a lot about idols in the church for a reason. It is very easy for me to put my job on a pedestal. It's very easy to find my worth in being a CPA. It's also very easy to put marriage on a pedestal when that's the thing I want so badly at this stage in my life.

Idols can be made out of our successes and our shortcomings. We have a lucrative job or boss we idolize over our Creator. We lack a relationship so we feel incomplete or unworthy. I think an argument could even be made that I have idolized Hallmark movies because I see the perfect meet-cute[27] and the ultimate happiness they find and I want that for myself to the point so much that I could cry after it's over. This may be a bit of a stretch as far as idols go, but the point is that the process of idol-making is sneaky.

One of my biggest fears in writing what I'm about to write is that my parents or grandparents feel guilt for my short-sightedness. So please let me be very clear in saying that this is my personal problem that began and grew as a result of my lack of understanding and my shortcoming and my sin. Not my parents, not my hometown, not any other person but me.

My idol was perfection.

I allowed my perception of how everyone looked at me to dictate how I lived my life for many years. My parents raised me to be a good, responsible, and kind person, but I took it too far. I stretched beyond the demands of a "good" person and turned that standard into perfection I believed I had to live up to. Y'all, perfection and image can be the sneakiest of idols. This idea that I had to look this way or act that way because I was a church goer or Senior Class President or because I was the daughter or granddaughter of so-and-so (remember how I talked about needing to be a "goodie-good" growing up?) became the end-all-be-all for my decision making.

My choices were no longer decided by asking, "Will this decision honor God?" or "Is this where God is leading me?" They were decided on "What will people think of me if I don't run for class president?" or "What will my boss think of me if I don't do my job without messing up?" or my personal favorite "What will people think of my family or my firm if my mistakes or unkind comments are public?"

I'm embarrassed just writing all of that, but it's the truth. For so long, I took people's perception of me and people's perception of the people I'm connected to and placed the burden of looking perfect firmly on my weak shoulders. Can you imagine how that turned out? You don't have to because I'm going to tell you: not perfect. I know you're just as shocked as I am, but my choices inevitably included quite a few mistakes. My job was not at all done perfectly, not even close. My words were not always kind. For a while, I allowed this perfection issue to keep me so burdened and bogged down with the weight of my mistakes until I physically and emotionally couldn't handle it anymore.

I distinctly remember breaking down on a couch in the lobby of my church, weeping to the Young Adult Pastor at the time about how I was feeling so angry about something and couldn't keep it to myself any longer. I was allowing this anger to crush me on the inside because "good people don't get angry." Just thinking about this moment brings me to tears because I had believed this for so long I didn't even realize in the moment how crazy it sounded. I had turned perfection into such an idol I didn't even realize the effect of such a harsh way of living until I had that breakdown.

This is the thing about idols, and when I say they are often sneaky it is because this is how they have presented themselves in my life. We don't have many golden calves to bow down to these days, but we do have image, perfection, expectations, marital status, money, careers, and a host of other platforms idols can be built upon when we forget these things are labels and not identities.

We often don't even realize these idols are being built in our lives until we wake up one day and we spend more time and energy maintaining our job status than our relationship with Christ or we start doubting His goodness when it seems like He is withholding something from us. This is why we must be so diligent in seeking Christ and in re-establishing our connection with Him each and every day of our lives. When our identities are rooted in Christ, we can live our labels, including our work, without living out of them because as Tim Keller writes in his book *Every Good Endeavor*, "The gospel frees us from the relentless pressure of having to prove ourselves and secure our identity through work, for we are already proven and secure."[28]

In case you missed that, we don't have to prove ourselves. Our worth and our dignity are not based on the labels we place on ourselves or those other people have placed on us. When our identities are secure in Christ, that security in Christ allows us the freedom to share all of us without fear of letting labels become idols. But just because we don't let these things determine our worth doesn't mean they don't define us in some form. I know this is not at all a popular sentiment, what with the whole "my past does not define me" mantra, but sit with me here for a moment…

I have a strong work ethic. My work ethic was exemplified by my parents and my family growing up. I knew the value of money and the responsibility to use it wisely and work hard for it. I value my work ethic, but this doesn't mean I overemphasize it to feeling as though I have to work hard until the job is done perfectly or else I'm a lazy, good for nothing human being.

I am a Tennessean. That doesn't mean I am a better person than someone from Alabama (but - Go Vols), but it means being from Tennessee has helped shape the defining moments of my life. The way I was raised, the people I grew up with, the sports teams I cheer on week after week have all been partly defined by the fact I am from and continue to live in Tennessee.

I am a CPA. Me claiming that title doesn't mean I find my worth in adding those three letters to the end of my name, but they tell the story of years of hard work to get an undergraduate and graduate degree and pass four of the hardest tests in the business industry. My CPA certification defines me professionally.

I am a sister. Me being a sister doesn't make me a better person than someone who is an only child (it may actually be the opposite because girls can be real mean to each other). Me being a sister defines my childhood. I grew up with two little brats (kidding) following me around and trying to mimic me for many years until the blessed day we began to grow into our own selves. I was the responsible sister, the one who had to make good decisions and be a good role model because, as the oldest, I was setting the standard. Being a sister (more specifically, being the oldest sister) taught me the value of my actions, words, and choices because those actions, words, and choices would likely be copied, even down to the simple act of when you could start shaving your legs.

I am a brain surgery survivor. This one is tough, and I don't really know how I would even find my worth in this one unless we consider how it destroyed my view of worth, but it definitely does define me. I'm not stuck on this situation and forever saying, "Poor me, look at this super painful thing I went through," but this identifying mark represents a time in my life where I was in the darkest of moments, where I saw the darkest side of myself and the ugliest parts of my heart, and where I found the brightest view of the power of God that I have ever experienced. This experience defines a turning point in my life, where everything truly did seem worthless compared to knowing Christ as my Lord.[29]

I want to take a moment and say your pain is not to be diminished. Your pain is your pain and your struggles are your struggles. They are real and they are hard. In the midst of your grief, allow yourself to grieve. In the midst of your illness, allow yourself to recognize this is not what you planned for and this is not what you want and this just plain sucks. When you find yourself in the dark or in the desert, allow yourself to acknowledge these are hard places and for this reason you do not have to pretend to be happy about being here.

Acknowledge your pain for what it is: hard and messy and difficult and painful. But please, please, please, also acknowledge the presence of God. Recognize His hand resting over you, His peace living inside of you, and His strength working in your weakness. This struggle and these desert days are a part of your story. Whether you like it or not, they are a part of you now. They will be (or maybe already are) defining moments you will one day look back on and either say, "This is where everything went wrong. This is where my life was flipped upside down and I never recovered," or "This is where everything went wrong. Where my life was flipped upside down and I found that God still works when the ceiling becomes the floor. This was the moment I experienced the sustaining power of the Lord that leads me on even today."

When you accept the defining moments of your life, I hope you see the Lord in all of them. I hope you see His strength in the struggle, His grace in the grit, and His joy in the journey. I hope you accept the moments which led you here. We don't have to be over-the-moon happy about the events that happened in our lives, because some things are just bad and dark and scarring in more than just the physical sense. I do think we need to process what we have gone through so we see them as part of our story. Our stories are unique and made up of so many pieces for the Lord to work together to show the people around you that you are a child of God without having to even say the words.

So when I say I'm a CPA and writer born and raised in Tennessee who loves to drink white mochas and watch hockey games, that's who I am. I am all of these titles and more, because the Lord made me. He created me to be who I am. He granted me the brainpower (albeit a bit too large of a brain, according to my surgeon) to complete my degrees and pass the CPA exam. He planted a streak of creativity in me which allows me to write and process or make sense of things using words swirling around senselessly within my mind. He knit me together, so He knew my brain placement would one day cause a problem, and He filled me with enough of His strength and grace to endure that. He built my taste buds so it comes as no surprise to Him I crave white mochas Every. Single. Day.

When asked the question of who I am or when asked to tell about myself, my faith is a big part of who I am, but the expressions of my faith complete the picture. As A.W. Tozer once wrote, "Within him was God; without, a thousand gifts which God had showered upon him."[30] So I will tell of my faith, but I will also tell of the creativity and the book-smarts and the passions that have been given to me by the source of my faith. I will tell of Christ and of the saving power I have found in my life, and I will tell of how I love hockey and am currently living on my own as a single gal. I will tell of my family, of my hometown, of my work, because ultimately each of these things are a gift from the Lord and a tool He has used to shape me into the young woman I am today. My identity is only found in Christ, but that identity is expressed in every part of me.

My prayer for you is my prayer for myself. That we as professionals, as believers, as Gospel-minded individuals, and as unique creations of the Almighty God, would embrace our history. That we would celebrate the way that our brains work differently, the different creative outlets we enjoy, the variety of professions and positions that the Lord has crafted us to do well. I pray we would recognize the defining moments of our lives and stop feeling guilty for answering the question "Who are you?" with anything other than "I am a child of God." Yes, we are children of the Most High God and I believe this should be included in the answer, but He has created us to express that kinship in a variety of ways, all of which display His creativity and His care for each of us personally.

My prayer is we would not allow our identifying marks to become idols in our lives, thinking of the marks more than the Maker. I pray we wouldn't let the seeming lacking areas of our life dictate our worth and our dignity, and we would recognize our value as image-bearers of a God who longs to be our Lord. I pray we wouldn't be buried under the weight of measuring up to an image or an idol outside of who we are in Christ.

I pray we would not only recognize our life moments and the attributes of ourselves are defining, but also recognize we have the power to choose *how* these moments will define us. In our creation story, we were given the power of choice. To choose Jesus or to choose the world. To choose to binge watch every season of Downton Abbey in four weeks or choose to study a book of the Bible in that same time. To choose to invest in healthy relationships or to allow the fallen human nature to dictate our decisions. To choose the chocolate bar or choose the strawberry ice cream (that's healthy, right?).

We have the choice of letting our moments be defined by our own strength (or lack thereof) or letting those moments be defined as God shining down on us with undeserved favor or unfailing rescue. We have the choice of letting trauma and pain and loss rule our thoughts and hearts for the rest of our lives or taking those struggles and searching for God in the midst of them, searching for the goodness we know He will bring into them, leaning into the growth we know comes from troubled times, and standing on the other side with a testimony of how the Lord can and does work. We can choose to give our struggles to God and watch Him turn them into a story He will use for His glory. We can choose how we will answer the question: Who am I?

AS YOU GROW UP: A LETTER FROM CHRISTA VANZANT

Growing up in a small Oklahoma town with small thinking did not equip me for the perils of life. As I grew older, I compared myself to everyone and never felt I measured up. This comparison created a self-imposed identity crisis which lasted into my adulthood. It created so much fear, anxiety, and perfectionism, and contradicted everything I knew about my Creator and what He wanted me to believe about myself.

What I wish I'd known then was that the voices that told me I was "less than" were from the enemy. It was a designed attack because the Devil knew who I was to become and was on a mission to stop the destiny and purpose for my life. I wish I would have relaxed and rested into God's version of me earlier. He created me, and I simply needed to rest in Him and trust the workmanship.

I pray you would remember to find your rest in the Lord, relaxing into who HE says you are and ignore the voices contradicting His word. Focus in on the vertical relationship with God, and HE will help you with the horizontal relationships in your life. HE will guide you. It is not our self-reliance or our efforts which define our success; it is through HIM and in HIM where we find our purpose and path.

CHAPTER 7
Crack in the Brick

"My job cannot be my security, and money cannot be my safety net." I can't count the times I've had to repeat this to myself over the past three years. These are good things on their own, but they are not sturdy enough to catch me when I fall.

When I was younger, I had this blanket. You know the knitted blankets with stitchings you could stick your fingers in between? This was my security blanket (literally). I did not sleep without it for years, and it seemed almost an unconscious thought to stick my little fingers through the stitching when I was nervous or scared or even just for the heck of it. For some reason, this blanket made me feel safe. If I was covered by this blanket and could tangibly feel the loose stitching that told me it was my blanket, the monster under the bed and the coyotes outside the house couldn't get me. The problem with constantly tearing apart the stitching of your favorite blanket, however, is that you start to create a hole that, if left unchecked, can become large enough to slip your entire body through.[31] As much as I loved this blanket, over the years, it became nothing more than an outline of string with a massive hole in the middle, torn up so much it could really no longer be called a blanket.

Fast forward about fifteen years, and I had a real job and a set income. I was well-suited for the position, getting along with my coworkers, and skilled in the actual work. In short, I was good at my job and this was affirmed by my bosses, so I felt safe. I don't think I realized it when I first started working, but from the time I accepted the job and walked in the door, my world felt a little more secure because I thought my long-term plan and financial peace was set. I was going to work there for at least seven years or so, maybe more or maybe less depending on when I moved back home. I was going to establish myself at this firm and rise quickly through the ranks. I was going to work, and I was going to make good money, enough money to support myself and save a pretty penny along the way. My job wasn't going away anytime soon; it was only going to get better, or so I thought. However, just as with my blanket all those years ago, the more I relied on the job as my security, the more I became willing to work longer hours or take on bigger projects to help me appear invaluable to the firm, something started to tear apart. Except this time the thing being torn apart wasn't the job; it was me.

Having a job is a necessary part of life, and a workplace can be a wonderful space to connect with people and support yourself financially. But y'all, no matter how safe it feels, no matter how invaluable we think our job might be, the job itself is not a fail-proof security blanket. The job might hold up initially, but it will ultimately not provide the security that our hearts and minds desperately long for.

The truth is, jobs fail. Businesses fail. Health fails. Why? We're human. Businesses are run by humans. Humans, as we see time and time again in Scripture and in our own lives, are fallible. We make mistakes. We fall short. We make decisions which could end relationships or job tenures or even businesses as a whole. Situations outside of our control can set up camp in our lives and take the job from us. We could lose the job or the income because of another person's actions.

So where do we as humans, as employers, as employees, as women, as children of the Most High God find our security? As the song goes, "in Christ alone." Christ and Christ alone will be our stronghold and our security, because true security is found only in the thing that will not fail to be secure on its own.

Let me say it in a different way: our craving for long-term security will only be satisfied in the God Who will never fail. The God Who will never abandon us. The God Who promises to be our Safe Place and our Shelter from the storms. He has promised to hide us under His wings when the battles are waged in our lives. When we need more than ever to feel secure on the inside as the world around us seems to be reeling, God's promises stand strong and immovable.

I have always loved the classic hymns. I grew up in a small town Southern church where the only music played outside the hymnal was during vacation Bible school. These hymns—many of them written years and years prior to my singing them as a child—always sounded so beautiful to me. There is something about the purity of the words, the care with which each word seemed to be placed where it was in the tune, and the timeless truths belted out by all who lifted their voices made me feel so connected with the God we would sing about.

Two songs in particular find their way into my head as I struggle with finding my security in Christ. The first, a newer song, "In Christ Alone" says this:

> *"In Christ alone, my hope is found,*
> *He is my light, my strength, my song.*
> *This Cornerstone, this solid Ground*
> *Firm through the fiercest drought and storm.*
> *What heights of love, what depths of peace*
> *When fears are stilled, when strivings cease*
> *My Comforter, my All in All*
> *Here in the love of Christ I stand."[32]*

The second hymn, "My Hope is Built on Nothing Less" goes like this:

> *"My hope is built on nothing less*
> *Than Jesus' blood and righteousness*
> *I dare not trust the sweetest frame*
> *But wholly lean on Jesus' name*
> *On Christ the solid Rock I stand*
> *All other ground is sinking sand."*[33]

These two hymns point back to the final words of Jesus in His Sermon on the Mount. Both hymns point to hope built firmly and only on the foundation of Jesus Christ. Jesus is the Cornerstone, the solid Ground, and the solid Rock. He is the source of security we desperately need in the drought and the storm and even when life is sweet because "all other ground is sinking sand."

As we lay our foundation and set the ground on which we will build our personal and professional lives, I hope we'll remember the words of Jesus in Matthew 7:24-27 (NLT):

> *"Anyone who listens to my teaching and follows it is wise, like a person*
> *who builds a house on solid rock. Though the rain comes in torrents and*
> *the floodwaters rise and the winds beat against the house, it won't collapse*
> *because it is built on bedrock. But anyone who hears my teaching and*
> *doesn't obey it is foolish, like a person who builds a house on sand. When*
> *the rains and floods come and the winds beat against that house, it will*
> *collapse with a mighty crash."*

Jesus wants us to build our lives on Him. He knows how important it is not only to our lives on earth but also to our eternal lives that we build on the solid Rock. He even tells us exactly how to do it: "Listen to my teaching and follow it." We have to listen to His teaching, read the Word, know the Word, and listen to the stirring of the Spirit as

He reveals His plans for us. Then we have to follow His teaching, obey the Word, and follow His leading in our lives.

So let me ask you this: Is your house built on the Rock or on your salary?

After watching so many HGTV episodes, I personally feel qualified to talk about home renovation like an expert. I can throw out things like, "This space would really open up if we just knock down this one wall" or, "Add some shiplap" or, "Gut the house and start over." One of the most terrifying sentences to hear in this scenario is, "There's a crack in the brick." One thing I know about this statement, purely from watching these TV shows, is that most of the time these cracks are related to the foundation. Most likely, this is a result of an improper support system for the foundation when the house was first built (the last part was courtesy of my multi-talented dad).

If the cause is improper build, the problem is usually not immediate. It could also take anywhere from ten to fifty years for the truth to rear its ugly head. The time it takes for the crack to appear depends partly on how the foundation settles and largely on how much weight is being supported by the foundation. Regardless of the timeline, there is now a crack in the foundation which could be devastating.

When I was asking my dad about this, I didn't even tell him what I was writing about, but this idea of weight being the biggest factor for how long the foundation would hold up was one of the first points he made. As he spoke these words, I found myself wearing a small smile because I knew immediately the good Lord above was speaking through those words.

Y'all, just as the foundation of a home will break apart faster when it bears more weight, the more we try to build our lives on anything other than Jesus Christ, the faster we will fall. When we allow our jobs or our health or our relationship status or our zip code to be the security we lean more heavily on, the cracks in our lives will reveal themselves and prove to be even more devastating than a crack in the brick.

Let me ask again: Who/what are you building your life on?

Whatever your answer is, if it's not Jesus, your life will not stand. Just like the folks who hear the dreaded words of cracked brick, our foundation apart from Jesus may stand for many years, but ultimately it will crack. The underlying issue will eventually present itself as unavoidable, and when it does, we will have to choose to either turn back to Jesus and allow Him to help us reset our foundation or crumble like the house built on sand.

After being in my first job full-time for eight months, I was feeling great. I loved the atmosphere, I loved the people, and while I don't know many tax accountants who could say they love taxes, I honestly enjoyed the work. Life was good, but a big part of my heart was starting to believe life was good because I was increasingly reliant on my job and the success that had so far come with it. Yes, I love the Lord and I believe He provided me this job and the abilities to be successful in it, but it was very easy to start leaning more on my desk than on the infallible promises of the Lord. With every success and all the positive feedback I received, my heart leaned into my job while my spirit struggled with knowing I was entering dangerous territory. As my job became more and more crucial to my feeling safe, the unrest within me only grew stronger.

When the storms of life raged, all the little tears that began as unrest became an all-out hole and I fell straight to the ground. I remember the day in vivid detail, though the days that followed over the next few months are a blur. Unknown to me at the time, my brain had decided it was time to let me know that it wasn't exactly sitting in the right place in my head. Instead of being where it should be, my brain was resting a tad too close to my spinal cord, so with every beat of my heart, my brain was creating a kind of compression chamber at the base of my head where pressure was being built with every beat. As you can likely imagine, the result was excruciating pain, and while I'm told the condition is something I've had since birth, the symptoms only then presented themselves.

Here I was, a newly licensed CPA with a pretty great job, feeling as though the ground just fell out from beneath my feet on a Monday afternoon in March in the middle of tax season. The following months were full of pain stronger than I have ever experienced and ended with a brain surgery to relieve the pressure and give my brain room to breathe accompanied by a doctors note saying I couldn't work for the next ten weeks.

While the work of the Lord through this experience was perfectly present and many lessons were learned through it all (stay tuned for more of those lessons), I want to use this story here to show how important it is for us—as believers and children of God—to rely on our Father above everything this world can offer. I lost sight of this important lesson, and when my job was taken away for two and a half months, I felt like my security blanket had been stolen off of me and I was a prime candidate for the TV show *Naked and Afraid*.

Keep in mind I had only been working full-time for eight months. It can happen so quickly and so easily, and because I had relied more and more on my job over those eight months, when I couldn't work, I felt lost. It was so easy to start feeling safer in my job than in my faith. When I was given positive feedback and comments about my potential, my level of security got a boost. When the feedback didn't come my way when I thought it should, I found myself in a downward spiral of doubt and anxiety.

I joke about being naked and afraid, but that is quite literally how I felt. I had lost my security blanket, the thing I thought wouldn't end until I decided to leave the job, and I was afraid of what it would mean for my career track if I didn't work for ten weeks. Would I come back and everyone had passed me in the climb up the ladder? Would I lose my ability to work at the same pace and skill level I was accustomed to? Would everyone treat me differently and think I was less capable because I had brain surgery?

The good news is, while I can definitely say I fell through the cracks in my foundation during this time, the cracks were revealed before the whole house collapsed. If you're having trouble understanding where I was at in this moment, picture this: There had been a few soft spots in the hardwood floor for a while. I saw them but just stepped over them and continued on my way for months, ignoring the problem and thinking, "It's fine, I can handle this." Then one day, the soft spots caved in and I found myself falling through the new hole in the floor. The house (my faith in God) was still standing but I could no longer pretend everything was okay.

Now I saw the problem, and I could start fixing it. This was the point where God, with all of His kindness and promises, bundled me up and held me close. I frequently shared my concerns and my fears with Him, and each time He listened to the fears trying to tie up my thoughts and rather than condemning me for my unbelief and all the time I had leaned more heavily on my job, He pulled me closer to Himself as He reminded me again of how secure His promises are to me (and you). He gently worked in my heart during this time, knowing, as the Wonderful Counselor would, my heart couldn't take much more. Was the pain I was experiencing terrible? Yes. Did I find myself on the slippery slope of depression? Yes. But the Lord held me tighter under His shelter with each slip of my foot and each beat of my heart. With every workless day, He was resetting my foundation.

I don't want you to hear me wrong, I still like being part of a team and an organization that works together to accomplish something. I still like working, but more than wanting to work, I want Jesus. I *need* Jesus. Jobs may come and go, but the Word of the Lord endures forever.[34]

Since this revelation, I have worked with Jesus to keep my foundation strong. Where I once allowed my focus on work to act as a catalyst that allowed work to climb into the top priority spot in my life, I have prioritized Jesus. Where I at one point would claim church could be missed if I needed to work, I made it clear to my managers I would not work during the time I needed to be at church. Let me point out now that in making it clear to my managers I did so in a respectable way (for the most part). I would work extremely hard and longer if needed on the other six days of the week, but on the seventh day, when I needed to be in church, when I needed the Word of God and the community of believers to pour into me to refresh my heart and mind, I would not work.

This is what I want you to understand about security, and what I'm continuing to understand by the grace of our God. He alone is capable of meeting every need we have. He wants our trust. He jealously craves our attention, so much so that if we are finding security in something other than Him, there is a good chance He will allow that blanket to fall through our fingers until we once again find ourselves holding onto Him. Out of love, He will bring us back to Himself. Psalm 91:1 (NLT) says, *"Those who live in the shelter of the Most High will find rest in the shadow of the Almighty."* When we choose to live in the shelter of His secure promises, He has promised rest. Can your job promise that?

If you're wrestling with where your source of security is right now, remember it all starts with the foundation. If you feel as though you've exhausted your current foundation and you're trying to find how to rebuild on something more secure, Jesus can help with that. He wants to help.

Please choose to build your foundation on Him by learning from Him: His word, His promises, His love. Respond in obedience. Follow Him. Follow His Word. Build your life, every part of your life, on the only One who is strong enough to face whatever might come your way. You might still have to deal with asbestos or having to rewire all the electrical in your house, but you can rest easy knowing your house will stand.

AS YOU GROW UP: A LETTER FROM SIMI JOHN

I remember when I started working as a physical therapist, I felt like I had to know all the answers to every question my patients asked. I spent so much time trying to talk and over-explain everything even when I truly didn't know the answer. Part of me felt like I needed to prove to them that I was smart and deserved to be there. Growing up in the Indian culture of shame and honor, education was of high value and failure was not an option, so I was trained to perform and achieve. The problem is when you become an adult and get a job or have kids, there is no real prize or grade to let you and everyone else know you are doing a good job. You're left with this nagging feeling of wanting to be seen and acknowledged for what you do, and when that doesn't happen, you are left feeling dissatisfied.

It took me a long time to realize as a physical therapist, the greatest gift I can give my patients is a listening ear. They may not remember everything I explained to them in regards to their deficits and functional goals, but they will remember how I made them feel. When I really understood this truth, I was able to walk in confidence and say the words, "I don't know." I was trying to be wise not admitting these three words for so long in my career, but it was wisdom which taught me to say them without fear or shame.

I wish someone had told me early in my career that I don't have to know all the answers or strive to prove myself all the time. I have a doctoral degree from a top university in America. I am smart and I am a good therapist. I needed to let those facts sink in and accept that validation for myself and not seek it from others. It is not the role of other people to make me feel approved and accepted; that is giving others too much power over me and putting too much pressure on them. How do we get to this place of contentment in our identity? We go to the Word of God, where we find our identity as a Child of God, approved and accepted because of the blood Jesus spilled on our behalf. When we abide in this truth, we no longer have to strive to achieve or perform to be perfect. We already have the highest honor, and we could never earn it nor do we deserve it. We can rest and allow Jesus to fill our cups and the overflow which comes forth is one of service to those around us. It is no longer for their approval or our own glory, but a gift of what we have been freely given.

I pray as you grow up you will find your contentment in Christ alone. Your dream job will never satisfy, marriage and children will never provide fulfillment and no initial behind your name will give you the identity Jesus paid to give you. I hope you will rest in the finished work on the cross and not in the work of your own hands.

CHAPTER 8
Love the Dust

Okay, y'all. I want to change gears for a second. What happens when we're a year into our job and no longer feel like celebrating? What happens when we've set our foundation and we know who we are but the dust settles back into view after our deep cleaning? What happens when the "dust" is ordinary life and the "dirt" looks a lot like imperfections in your job position, or your relationships, or your personal mindset?

Before I continue, I want to make something extremely clear: no person or job or employer or relationship is perfect. Nothing is perfect outside of Christ himself. My intent isn't to criticize the imperfections of another because, as much as I like to think so, I am definitely not perfect. The Good Book makes very clear we are all sinners who have fallen short of the glory of God[35] and before we point out the speck in another's eye, we need to remove the log in our own.[36]

With these thoughts in mind, my goal is to focus on our reaction to the problems present in every workplace and every heart, not on the problems themselves. As with every chapter in this book, the stories are from my point of view and my responses (good and bad) all wrapped up in trying to review each part through the eyes of a gracious God who sees past every imperfection to love the soul behind them.

God's view of the Church as the Body of Christ is the central focus of 1 Corinthians 12 . The body is made up of many parts, each unique and each important. In the Church, the Body is united in one common goal: to further the Kingdom of God on this earth. This chapter says (in part):

> *"There are different kinds of gifts, but the same Spirit distributes them. There are different kinds of service, but the same Lord. There are different kinds of working, but in all of them and in everyone it is the same God at work."*[37]

Whatever your work is, God is in it. Whether in the Church, in the workplace, in the home, or on the battlefield, God is working both in you and through you. These verses bring me immense hope and encourage me to look towards the source of any kind of work as a member of the Body of Christ. They release the expectations I place on myself, the ones I perceive others are placing on me, and the ones I place on others. They tell me the same God is working in every place and every heart. Even when I can't see how, even when I don't feel it, even when everything and everyone seems negative and difficult, God is still at work.

As a new-ish employee, I find most people, myself included, come in with both guns blazing, ready to work hard and change what's not great and empower everyone to be the best and so on and so on. We tend to get caught up in everything we want to do right now, all at once, because we're excited. Being excited is not a bad thing, but when the reality sets in that you can't change or fix everything you want to, it's hard to cope when coming off the buzz of a new job. I think the same principle applies to relationships. We begin a new relationship excited about the possibilities and then somewhere along the way we begin to settle into the realization that people are flawed.

When the newness starts wearing off, we have a choice to make. Do we buckle our seat belts and keep moving forward together, or do we throw our hands up and walk away from people or jobs because it's just too hard? This is the question I want us to consider in this chapter because it's something we have faced or will face. There will come a time when our workplaces or our homes or our lives won't look as good as they once did. Our nameplates sit covered in dust that seems to pile up overnight. Our dishes pile up in the sink. Our problems pile up by the day. When we find ourselves here, how will we respond?

We must cling to the promise that God is at work and He has placed us where we are with greater intentionality than we can understand in the moment. This is what most people tell us when we ask questions like this, and I absolutely agree. I understand the importance of recognizing the Lord's intentionality in placing us where we are, but my question has often been about how we tangibly live out our Kingdom calling when it feels more like damage control. How do we respond to the dust that settles at work or the dirt of sin that exists in imperfect people?

At the end of 1 Corinthians 12—a chapter telling us of the uniqueness of each member of the body of Christ and the different gifts and acts of service and works God is in, a chapter that promotes unity among people—we find this verse:

"But now let me show you a way of life that is best of all."[38]

Do you know what comes next? Love. Love is the answer. When the going gets tough and the issues seem to get messier, we show love. When we live and work without love, we are only a noisy cymbal; we are nothing and we gain nothing. When we love, when we live in the way of life that is "best of all," we are patient and kind. We are not jealous or boastful or proud or rude. We keep no record of wrongs. We rejoice in truth. We don't give up. We don't lose faith. We have hope. We endure through every circumstance. [39]

In my final season in public accounting, saying the work environment was difficult would be an understatement. The fault does not belong to any one person. We were going into our busiest time of year with more work and more hours and less people and a brand-new set of laws to follow in preparing income tax returns. Who knew there would come a season where we would re-prepare the same tax return three times in the span of a month because of changing IRS guidance? Basically, it was the perfect storm of circumstances, and we all struggled as a result.

A year before, we had an incredible team made up of extremely intelligent people who genuinely were an encouragement to me. When I say encouragement, I'm talking about people who literally gifted me their PTO to make sure my finances were sufficient when I was out of work for ten weeks on short-term disability. People who cared not only for the well-being of the firm but for the well-being of the people who made up the firm. At least that's what my perception was.

However, in the months leading up to this specific tax season, four people left. When the first coworker left, I honestly wasn't that surprised because I had seen how undervalued this person had been. They truly went above and beyond to get the work done, and that drive was taken advantage of. Maybe not intentionally, but it happened nonetheless, and so they left. In the process of turning in a two-week notice, this person was asked to leave in a way I felt was extremely disrespectful.

I have never been one to accept the "this is common practice" answer, especially when it doesn't seem right. I've also never been very good at keeping my mouth shut when I see disrespect, or when I perceive something was disrespectful. Down to the basics of my personality, my goal is to do things right, to be respectful, and to be good. When I see something I believe is wrong or disrespectful, my words and often my facial expressions get the best of me. In this particular situation, I was asked my opinion on how things happened, so I gave it.

Recognizing the person asking was one of my superiors, I (as calmly as I could) said "I think that was the most disrespectful thing I have seen happen here." Obviously this was not taken as well as I had hoped, and I began to receive a lesson on public accounting, two lessons actually. Neither of which did anything to ease my frustration.

In my effort to try to keep my job and not let words fly out of my mouth I couldn't take back, I quite literally had to bite my tongue to keep myself silent. I'm still convinced it was by the grace of God I didn't say anything, but I'm also pretty sure my facial expression gave away a little of what I was thinking.

The damage was done in my mind, and while I didn't respond immediately, I couldn't forget that moment. I can still remember it vividly. Over the next month, three more people gave their notice and left, leaving us down four people and going into the busiest time of year. I don't want to make it seem like my bosses were horrible people, because they weren't and they still aren't. I also don't want to make it seem like I handled the situation better than I did, because I most definitely did not. The point of me telling you this is not to bash the people who saw enough potential in me to give me my first full-time job. The point is my response to this problem was not great. As a believer and a member of the body of Christ, I am to love first and foremost. But I didn't do that.

In the months which followed and even to the day I turned in my notice, I held a grudge. I let those two little lessons linger. I didn't confront my boss later about how I was feeling about that comment, but I did talk about what happened to other people in the office.

I am not proud of this. I should have had a conversation with this member within a few days. I knew it was best to not immediately respond because I don't think I should ever talk when I'm in the grips of rage, but I should have talked to this person immediately when the tension dissolved. I shouldn't have brought up that conversation to other people who weren't there that day. I shouldn't have spread that comment to anyone whose ears didn't hear it when it happened. I spread that bug of disrespect instead of rejoicing only when truth won out, and I have felt so much guilt over it.

Where I should have extended grace and kindness, I extended judgment. Where I should have cleared the air and moved on, I held on to the hurt and justified my response as I closed myself off to any relationship. I acted in direct opposition to 1 Corinthians 13:5 which says, "*love keeps no record of wrongs.*" I forgot every person in my firm was as much an image-bearer of God as I was and God was at work in them too. I didn't curse or hate anyone, but I also didn't forgive, support, or build up as we are called to do. What could have been an incredible opportunity to share the grace of God and the love as defined by Paul in 1 Corinthians 13 was wasted. I think this is what grieves me the most.

Throughout tax season, there was this dark cloud hovering over the department, and I hate to say I contributed to that. Over the next few months, words were exchanged, more disrespect was spread, communication broke down, expectations that were far from realistic were heaped upon us, lies spread through the office, the people in our department were about as transparent as a brick wall, encouragement and positivity were largely nonexistent, and we all suffered for it.

But even then, God had me there for a reason. While I contributed to part of the downfall, I also tried to do what I could to correct the problem when things got especially tough. After a certain point of negativity, I was just fed up with dreading work and resenting the people I worked with, so I started a "two positives" rule - much to the chagrin of my coworkers. When I heard a negative comment, the guilty party would tell me two positive things happening in their lives that day (or in general because some days it was difficult to find the positives). I'm convinced most of my coworkers hated me for it, and if you don't believe me, let me point out I was dubbed "Pepe Le Pew." For those who aren't familiar with that name, here's what Wikipedia says about Pepe:

"Pepe is constantly in search of love and appreciation. However, his offensive skunk odor and his aggressive pursuit of romance typically cause other characters to run from him." [40]

I don't know if this was a hidden way to tell me I smelled bad and I just didn't get it, but replace "romance" with "positivity," and this about hits the nail on the head for what I imagine those around me thought of my "two positives" rule. Regardless, it was those moments when we stopped working to force ourselves to find something positive that made many days bearable.

I've always been more on the optimistic side of things, but I won't say that I find positivity in every situation. Some situations truly are just bad, and I don't believe that we have to seem happy and bubbly and full of good cheer when those situations come our way. God gave us a wide range of emotions and He never intended for us to bottle up the bad ones and lock them in a box (as much as I tried to do so for many years).

We aren't called to be happy about the bad things, but I wholeheart-edly believe there is something to be found and celebrated in every single day God gives us breath. This is not a free ticket to embrace the "treat yo'self" lifestyle. Take it from my experience that treating yourself every day can be both expensive and dangerous to your self awareness and self-discipline (or lack thereof). However, we are given reason to celebrate something each day.

If you can't find reason in your current situation, here are a few things I strive to celebrate every day, especially on the hard days:

- His mercies are new every morning.[41] — Each day that we wake up, it's like the Lord looks at us, truly sees us, and says, "Okay, my child, I've given you another day. Yesterday is gone, forget about it, forgive those who hurt you yesterday and forgive yourself for the missteps you had. Today is new, and my mercy begins again right now. You are clean."

- Nothing can separate us from His love.[42] — Nothing. Nada. Niets. Nic. Pick whatever language you like. His love is here to stay.

- Where the Spirit of the Lord is, there is freedom.[43] — The Spirit is within us. When we accept the Spirit of God into our hearts, every chain of bondage is broken and every sin tripping us up is defeated. We are free, if only we accept it.

- We are known by God and He calls us by name;[44] our names are written on His hand.[45] — He sees every part of us, good and not so good. Even so, He chooses to call us to Himself.

- Jesus has defeated the grave and offered us eternal life;[46] we are saved by grace by faith.[47] — So much grace has been poured over us. We don't have to chase it, but we must choose it and embrace it.

If you need more reason to celebrate something every day, I'm happy to tell you there is so much more where these come from. Dive into the Word of God, learn more of what it looks like to live life in the way of love. Because work is not always easy. Work is not always exciting or dust-free or positive, and neither is the rest of life. Even in these moments, we have a choice to show love or to not show love.

Please choose to show love when the house is clean and work is great and when the house is dusty and work is hard. I have needed forgiveness for the moments I haven't shown love, and I have graciously been offered that forgiveness to move forward and make a different choice next time. While I no longer feel the guilt, I remember the result of not choosing love, and y'all, I don't want to be responsible for that. I don't want to be remembered as someone who judged harshly when I should have loved deeply. I find myself echoing the sentiments of Carey Scott when she says, "With the state of the world right now, I can't think of anything we need more than women who have the guts and grit to let their lives reek of Jesus."[48]

Whether you are living in the trenches of hard work or still loving the newness of what you're doing, remember Jesus. Remember love. Let your lives "reek of Jesus," of love Himself, as you remember God is working in you and and in your work. He has given you gifts and an opportunity to serve and the ability to work. Use these wisely for the Kingdom of God.

AS YOU GROW UP: A LETTER FROM HEIDI RASMUSSEN

I remember when I was a young Assistant Store Manager at JCPenney and my Store Manager had terminal cancer. I was overseeing everything and everyone. In my past, if an employee wasn't doing their job, I would just step in and do it for them. That was easy; I was capable, and I could do it.

During this time in my career, there wasn't enough of "me" to go around, so I was forced to have those tough, candid conversations with people. It was at this time I realized the importance of what I now call "business courage." It's easier to take on the "fixer" role and/or not say anything to someone who isn't performing to expectations. It is harder and takes more courage to tell someone they aren't meeting expectations and need to improve their performance.

As soon as I realized this and started to master the principles around conflict, it made a big difference in my career and gave me more peace in my life. I wish I'd known some of the basics I had to learn over time.

First, pray! If there is a difficult work conversation in your future or family tempers are flaring – whatever it is, prayer is the first step. Ask the Lord to direct your words, your thoughts, your actions and to remind you of His greatest commandment to love that other person (or people) as yourself.

Paul wrote to Timothy about sharing the good news: "For the Spirit God gave us does not make us timid, but gives us power, love and self-discipline." We use these same attributes in conflict situations: pray for boldness (not timidity), for power over your emotions and the situation, for self-discipline through the conversation and in the end, that He would love through you those with whom you're in conflict.

Second, plan! When dealing with a conflict situation, I hear many people say, "I just go with my gut." That's a recipe for disaster. After praying, I would encourage anyone to sit and plan for five minutes. You'd be surprised how long five minutes is and how valuable it is. Think about how you want the conversation to flow, what words you want to use, and what outcome you hope for. Those five minutes will make a HUGE difference in the end result.

When I'm suddenly thrown into conflict, here's my process...

- Prayer, even a fast one: "Lord, help me deal with this well and in Your power."

- A calm, confident voice: Raising our voice just makes others do the same. Keeping a calm low voice no matter how worked up others get is key to a good outcome.

- Listen, truly listen to the other person's concerns: You may hear something new that changes the conflict situation.

- Avoid fighting words: If you say, "I hear you have a problem with XYZ. What's going on?" versus "I think we're experiencing an issue with XYZ. Tell me more." Which of those responses will calm and which will agitate?

- Humor: Don't underestimate what well-placed humor can do in a tense situation. Humor is attractive. It endears us to people, it is calming, and it can change an entire interaction.

In the end, if you handled a conflict situation well and the other person doesn't like the outcome, realize it's OK if someone doesn't "like you."

As you're growing up, I pray you would remember you can avoid a lot of conflict—or make unavoidable conflict easier—by clearly setting expectations from the beginning. I used to wait too long to have candid conversations or confront people about their lack of performance. In my head, it was going to be a REALLY big difficult deal. Why? Because I hadn't told the person what I expected up front – and now I needed to tell them they weren't performing well.

In her book, *Dare to Lead*, Brene Brown says, "Clear is kind. Unclear is unkind." Here's a real-life example:

Scenario 1: You hire someone and 8 months later, realize they aren't a good fit, aren't performing well and you have to let them go. That is not going to be a fun conversation.

Scenario 2: You hire someone and review your expectations in the first week. You tell them that you'll review their performance against expectations in ninety days. Throughout the ninety days, you're meeting weekly and providing timely candid feedback. In this situation, you have a plan that's been shared with the other person and following up regularly, so the conversation is much easier and expected.

As Christians, we're called to be kind. It is kind to be clear about expectations and have candid conversations with people who aren't cutting it.

Finally, remember everything we do is a witness for Christ. If we handle conflict well—with professionalism, humor, confidence, self-discipline, grace and love—it's an honor to the Lord.

CHAPTER 9

Change is the Game

Change your personality. Change your accent. Change your expectations because they are just too high. Change your job. Change your church. Change your appearance. Change you.

Have you ever heard any of these? Before you stop reading, we aren't talking about these kinds of changes. I'm not going to play the part of the motivational speaker who yells from a stage, "You don't need to change! You're great the way you are! Everyone else just needs to accept you and stop trying to change you!"

I have no problem telling you that you are made in the image of God Who makes no mistake. He made every intricate detail of you with purpose and with a plan in mind. When someone tells you to change a superficial part of yourself, you don't have to listen because your beauty is rooted in the One whose image you bear and not the one who looks at you with a critical eye. But your heart…I can't tell you you don't have to change that. I can't tell you the way you think and the way you love are fine as they are.

You may not like this chapter if your reaction to change is negative, but buckle up, y'all. Here we go, because while I'm pretty sure I'm not the only one who doesn't feel all warm and fuzzy inside when the idea of change is brought up, change is essential to becoming who God created us to be.

Before I really jump in, I want to say up front: not all change is bad. When change comes in the form of an exciting new job, a new relationship, or the opportunity to relocate to a new place in the world, it can be exhilarating to step into a new thing affirmed by the Lord. I also believe the words of Paul who says, God will work all things for the good of those who love Him and are called according to His purpose.[49] I don't doubt God can take a change I see as bad and turn it into a part of my story used to bring goodness to my life and the grandest glory to Him. This whole book came out of such a change in my life. Even still, just thinking of or hearing the word "change" is often enough to bring a wave of fear and a flurry of rapid heartbeats that would seriously concern my cardiologist.

I don't know if you've ever watched Downton Abbey, but I can't help but think about the Crawley family when I think about change. If you've watched the show, you know the changes they faced and the struggle it was for them. If you haven't had the joy (and sometimes heart-wrenching tragedy) of watching the Crawley family, the series follows this affluent family as they struggle to navigate how to step into an entirely new way of life both during and post World War I.

Seeing this family face so many changes reminds me change is not a new concept. Contrary to the definition of the word, "change" itself is consistent. When it comes to our careers, our relationships, our life choices, and our church, we will see and experience change. Most of the time we will relate more to the frenzied response of Carson the butler, resisting change in any part because we don't know what it means or how it looks or how it will impact our comfort zone. We resist change because we aren't ready for it and because we think changing means we will lose part of ourselves.

The question isn't whether or not we'll be ready for change, because I can almost guarantee we won't be. The question is how do we thrive where we are right now when we know change could be right around the corner, ready to steal another piece of ourselves? How do we move beyond the memory of painful changes and let go of the fear that the next change might bring the same pain?

I want to share part of a blog post I wrote in March of 2019, a week before the one year mark of my own personal D-day. The day I first felt the pain that quickly crippled me in every sense of the word. As the first anniversary got closer on my calendar, I struggled to forget the life-changing moment I didn't see coming, and I allowed that struggle to open up a realm of fear I hadn't realized had taken hold in my heart.

> *"Today, I reflect on that day and I'm honestly brought to tears by what I didn't know then. I didn't know that in nine short days life as I knew it would be turned upside down. I didn't know that I was about to be brought to the end of my strength, my sanity, and frankly my ability to live. I didn't know that over the next few months I was going to find myself closer to the Lord of my heart than ever before out of pure desperation to grasp the one thing I knew would stay steady.*
>
> *I didn't know. Because it hadn't happened yet…I am finding fear creeping into my heart. Fear is reminding me of how oblivious I was to the pain that was so near to making it's presence known, and fear is telling me that it can happen again…"*[50]

I think sometimes we allow our fear of "bad" change to build up a lack of trust in what the Lord is trying to do in our lives. When this lack of trust builds up, we usually end up running before the Lord says to run, or we walk through a door not meant for us or we halt our steps and refuse to move forward because we've seen enough and don't think we can take any more. We allow our fear to determine our direction.

While my situation was not so much a choice as a reality, I did find myself choosing fear when looking to the future. If something like this could happen when I least expected it, how was I to live without bubble-wrapping my heart (and now my head) to protect it? How was I supposed to move forward when I had seen first-hand that life as I knew it could be stripped away in a moment?

I don't think I'll ever forget that fateful March evening because it happened so quickly and with zero warning. I won't forget how I was sitting at my desk at work around 5:00 p.m., gearing up for another long night (because tax season) when it felt as if a light switch was flipped on in my head. I won't forget the moments that followed with me trying to drive myself home and almost having to stop on the side of the road because I was having trouble keeping my eyes open due to the sheer level of pain I was experiencing. But most of all, I won't forget that at 3:00 p.m. that day, I had no idea what was about to happen.

Here's the important thing to remember: God knew. He knew exactly what was about to happen and how oblivious I was even minutes before the metaphorical switch was flipped. While the fear began to creep in as the one year anniversary of that day got closer, He knew I would need to be reminded of His protection, His deliverance, and His closeness. He knew I would need these words of Psalm 91 to serve as a reminder:

> *"Those who live in the shelter of the Most High will find rest in the shadow of the Almighty. This I declare about the Lord: He alone is my refuge, my place of safety; he is my God, and I trust him. For he will rescue you from every trap and protect you from deadly disease. He will cover you with his feathers. He will shelter you with his wings. His faithful promises are your armor and protection. Do not be afraid of the terrors of the night, nor the arrow that flies in the day. Do not dread the disease that stalks in darkness, nor the disaster that strikes at midday. Though a thousand fall*

at your side, though ten thousand are dying around you, these evils will not touch you…

The Lord says, "I will rescue those who love me. I will protect those who trust in my name. When they call on me, I will answer; I will be with them in trouble. I will rescue and honor them. I will reward them with a long life and give them my salvation."[51]

Unfortunately, we don't know when we'll next experience the terror of the night or the arrow that flies by day. Something could change our lives in a moment, day or night or noon. In every one of those changes, our faith and our declaration of "God be praised" must speak louder than our fear which tells us to run, to avoid, to hide, or to discount our faith.

When life throws a curve, we must remember who God is and what He has the power to do. I love this name found in Exodus: "Yaweh-nissi,"[52] which reminds us the Lord is our banner. He has surrounded us with His presence and declared us victorious, even in the moment we find ourselves with tears streaming down our face as we stare down what the most recent change means for our lives.

He never promises we can avoid change by following Him. In case you forgot, His very call to follow Him is a call to change. He calls us to take off our old nature and put on the new, the redeemed, the changed nature.[53] When we embrace this most important change in our lives, when we start allowing the Lord to transform our lives to look more like Him, when we are lovingly devoted to Him as written in Psalm 91, His promises to us are exactly what we need when facing the changes of life. His promises remind us of His nature and the victory extended to us as part of our new life. Go back and read the verses of Psalm 91 again, and focus on what the Lord promises He "will" do for us.

When we are in a season of change, we have a tendency to spiral in a frenzy of anxious thoughts but God has promised to give rest to those who live in His shelter, not in their heads.

When we find ourselves in an unexpected situation piercing our hearts with fear, He has promised He will rescue those who love Him, and He will protect those who trust in His name.

When we experience the trials and sorrows Jesus warns us of in John 16:33, God has promised His presence. He will be with us in the trouble and answer our every call.

When the storms rage in our lives, when we feel overwhelmed by the weight of a new job or a new struggle or the loss of a loved one, God has promised to be our shelter. He has promised to cover us.

Change can be hard, good, scary, difficult, wonderful, life-giving and life-taking, and many, many other descriptive words. In all things, in all changes, God's promises stand true. His promises are "Yes and Amen."[54]

We need to seek the Lord diligently as life changes for the better and the worse. We need to remember His promises. We will inevitably walk through a door not meant for us, and we may step outside of what God wants for us from time-to-time. But we need to remember that God is gracious and his mercies are new every morning. He is full of kindness and the second we recognize our misstep, He will lovingly guide us back to the one door through which He intended for us to walk. Remember, He will answer when we call, He will be with us in trouble, and He will rescue us, even when we need to be rescued from ourselves.

We can run until our feet give out, we can try to escape God and get away from the changes He wants to bring into our lives…and the Lord will be right there. He will be ready to pick us up and carry us back to the path He has for us, even if that path looks like Him putting us in the stomach of a fish for three days. Remember Jonah? Jonah had a clear direction from the Lord. He was told to go to Nineveh. Jonah was being called to something which would change the course of his life, and what did he do? He "got up and went in the opposite direction to get away from the Lord."[55]

Jonah had a clear directive from the Lord and went the opposite direction! God literally told him when he was to go and where he was to go to. Two thoughts come to mind when looking at Jonah's story. One: Jonah probably already had a plan for his life, and Nineveh was not part of that plan. There's a good chance he didn't want to change his plans. Two: Nineveh had a reputation bigger than Taylor Swift's album, and it wasn't a good one. He was probably afraid of what he would find when he got there.

I look at Jonah's story and I think, "How in the world could you know so clearly the change you were about to experience was part of God's plan and then not pursue it?" But honestly, I think we've all had our Jonah moments. We feel the Lord leading us to one job, but we choose a different job. We feel the Lord pushing us towards one location, but we fight to go towards another.

Growing up, I always swore up and down I was not leaving my hometown. I was born and raised there and by gosh, I was going to be there forever. I was going to leave only for a short stint at college, and then I was going to come right back to the safety of my home. During college, something in my heart began to shift. It wasn't that I liked the options offered in a bigger place, although I have grown extremely fond of Target being just a few minutes down the road. This shift was more than that. This was the Lord breaking apart the pieces of my heart so tied to my hometown that I wouldn't even entertain the thought of something different. Remember when I said we fear change because we might lose part of ourselves? I'm speaking to myself here, people.

I'd love to tell you I surrendered my plan immediately to the Lord and said, "Thy will be done," but that's not really what happened. Through the changes taking place in my heart, I chose to take internships in Nashville and thought, "This will be great experience, and this will all be used to make me a more well-rounded professional for when I go back home and start my own business." And then the internships in college turned into a full-time job offer…in Nashville.

By taking this job, part of me knew this is where God wanted me to be, and while it looked a lot different than I thought it would, I was trusting this life change was for the better. But a bigger part of me thought, "Okay God, we'll do this your way right now, so I'll work here in Nashville for a while and then I'll go back home because we both know that's where I belong."

Honestly, living outside of my hometown is still a change I struggle to accept. It's home. It's where my family is. It's the place which holds almost every memory of my first eighteen years. Much like Carson the butler in Downton Abbey, it scares me to give up what I've known all my life for a way of life I never even considered living. And y'all, I'm only living an hour and a half away. I can drive to my home home and be back to my now home (Nashville) in less than a day.

In reality, it's not much of a change, but to me, this one change is central to every part of my life. We shouldn't diminish the effect of change in each other's lives. My change may only mean seventy-five miles. Your change may be half-way around the world. Someone could look at these two scenarios and think your change is much more difficult than mine. Logistically speaking, they would be right. However, maybe you have been moving all your life and the thought of moving halfway around the world doesn't mean much because you're used to the change of scenery, while my move is the only real move I've made in my life. In both of our lives, we're experiencing change on different levels geographically, emotionally, and spiritually, so comparing the effects of our changes diminishes both of our responses.

It has taken me a full five years to write my next sentence and not want to weep at the reality of it: I don't think I'll move back to Lawrenceburg in the foreseeable future. I'm not prepared to say I absolutely won't because I don't know for certain where the Lord will lead me later on in life, but right now, Lawrenceburg is not where God needs me to be. I've been in Nashville full-time now for three years. I've grown more in these three years than I did in twice that many years in Lawrenceburg.

Here in Nashville, everything changed. My community of friends (for the most part) changed. My way of life changed from small-town speed to the hustle and bustle of the city. My routes changed from back roads to interstates (though I still find the back roads as often as I can). My choices and actions became a result of my own beliefs instead of the expectations of my family. Everything from the grocery store where I shop to the neighbors I have to the church I'm investing in, everything changed. Embracing this change has been so hard at times, but I know this is for my best and I am so thankful I chose to embrace the change I felt the Lord pushing me toward.

Would it have been easier to choose Lawrenceburg, to avoid the change or delay it a bit? Maybe. Yet if I had chosen like Jonah to go in the opposite direction, I would have missed out on some of the biggest blessings I've known in my life. I likely would have found myself in a situation where the consequences of stepping into something God never wanted for me became all too present and uncomfortable in my life. I don't think I would have found myself inside a fish like Jonah, but I might have found myself with a failing business or a broken relationship or some other situation forcing me to reevaluate my decision to follow the Lord's leading.

Thankfully, even if I did choose to run from the change the Lord was guiding me to, He doesn't give up when we choose the wrong direction. After finding himself back out of the fish and onto the sand, we're told this: "Then the Lord spoke to Jonah a second time: 'Get up and go to the great city of Nineveh, and deliver the message I have given you.' This time Jonah obeyed the Lord's command and went to Nineveh…"[56]

You may look at a choice you've made and think, "Man, this is *not* what God wanted me to do. I don't know how to get back on track after this." In that same moment, God can open a new road right where you are, a road not even on the map. These off-the-map roads are bumpy and rough in some places. They may not be easy to travel because God did not intend for you to travel down them, but in His mercy and grace, He made a way for you to get back to the road He created for you to walk down, the road He intended you to walk all along. Because He knew. He knew you were going to choose the way you did, and so He planned for the path to open up right as you recognized you were somewhere you weren't meant to be. He knew you would resist the change He wanted to bring you, and rather than giving up on you, He made a new way to bring you to it.

Our God will never give up on us. Just as He spoke to Jonah a second time, repeating the direction He intended Jonah to go, He speaks to us now. When we choose to run away or just initially not move at all, we feel the consequence of that choice and then we feel the grace of God which calls us once again, giving us a second chance to follow His lead. Aren't you thankful for a God Who believes in second chances?

Yes, change can be difficult and scary and lead us into places we never intended to go, but change is very much a part of God's plan for us. In both changes of my life, the loss of health and the finding of God's best for me in Nashville, I have seen the Lord work. I have even seen Him tie the two changes (bad and good) together as the community I found in Nashville became a God-given source of strength when the pain was too dark for me to handle on my own.

God knows what He is doing. We need change to grow. We need to be stretched and challenged and changed, or else we would be stuck in the same place forever. I wasn't created to stay in my own little ZIP code, and maybe you weren't, either. Change purposefully brought into our lives by God can be unpleasant and quite painful just as much as it can be restorative, but God is making all things new, including us.

Consider change as part of the refining work of the Lord in our lives. Whether planned by God or brought about by our own fear and lack of understanding, the Lord in His sovereign power and everlasting grace will meet you right where you are and draw you back to Himself and back to the life Jesus came to bring you. In the newness of our changes, we might find we haven't lost a piece of our true selves. We're becoming the person we were always meant to be.

AS YOU GROW UP: A LETTER FROM KIMBERLY MACNEILL

For the most part, I am a lover of change. For me, the saying "out with the old and in with the new" signals a call to adventure. I don't generally fear the unknown because I have found it mostly filled with potential and opportunity. I value learning and growing, and I know being open to change is required for both. As an ambitious professional, I understand change is necessary to move forward.

And while I can say I am a fan of the process and the good things change brings, I have also come to understand that change is messy. I used to think if I responded well and wisely to my circumstances and made the right choices, I could essentially control the outcome of any change. The sooner I got the change I wanted, the sooner I would find myself off on a new adventure once again. But as life experience teaches, this is not how it always happens. The fact is, sometimes change is disappointing; the bottom line is, sometimes change is down right difficult.

When you come to the more difficult seasons of change, there is something I want you to remember, something I wish I'd taken to heart sooner: God is for you.

God created you uniquely, loves you unconditionally, and designed you for a one-of-a-kind contribution to the world. He is the expert in the work of transformation and the ultimate CEO in the business of making all things new in your life. There is no season of change you will ever have to navigate alone. He knows more, sees more, and understands more about you and any situation in which you will find yourself. He will give you courage, fortitude, endurance, wisdom and faith as needed and in abundance. I want you to keep in mind that who you are on the inside is more important than what you do work-wise. Your character, the vibrancy of your heart, and the health of your soul matter much to God, more than any professional title or accomplishment. Along the way, there will be some changes which seem like setbacks to you, but you will later discover it was actually God intervening to protect you and direct you to a stronger foundation and future for your life. His ways, the changes He wants to make are always better. In the more difficult seasons of change, trust God's heart for you. And never, ever give up. You will feel like it sometimes, but don't do it. Remember: God is for you!

CHAPTER 10
Lord of My Planner

I hate waiting. I know what I want and I know when I want it. I'm a planner, and for a long time, if you had asked me what my five- or ten-year plan was, I could have given you bullet points for almost every year. I have dreams and goals; I see them in my future and I just want them to happen now. Right now! Writing this book has been a struggle for this very reason. I know what I want to say, but I can't say it all at once. I can't snap my fingers and have all the words perfectly lined up and structured in well-written sentences and perfectly concise points. Let's be honest; it doesn't matter how long I take to write these words, that is probably a long shot anyways.

As much as I don't love when timing doesn't work out like I've written it into my planner, if there's one thing I've learned over the years—especially over the past year—it's that God works on His own time and it is always, always better.

I didn't see myself being the girl who leaves her job after less than two years as a full-time staff to change career tracks. I didn't see myself ever writing a book in my life. I didn't see myself struggling to keep my eyes open and feet moving forward for almost three months because I was in so much pain. I didn't plan any part of the reality I'm currently living in.

I've been through the waiting and I've been through what feels like a fast-track to a new career. Both are difficult and both are extremely rewarding when I remember the faithfulness of God in the fast lane and the school zone alike. And while we're using driving analogies...

Have you ever been to the DMV? You know, the place where you sign in and take a number and sit for what feels like a whole year until you finally hear "forty-one" and then you have an internal dance party (or maybe an actual dance party if you're that kind of confident) because you know your number is next...and then you wait for another half hour and get kind of down again before you hear the number "forty-two" and you jump up and think, "Finally, it's my turn!"

I think life is a lot like the DMV. We have a tendency to create these expectations of how we think something is going to go, whether it's a college major, a job promotion, a relationship, or even a life plan. We think, "Okay, I'm going to go to the University of Tennessee and I will graduate in three years with a degree in Business Administration. Then I'm going to move back home and open my own business, but before I open the business, I'm going to get married. I won't have kids until the business is profitable, and then me and my husband will have two kids (boy first because that's important). And we'll live happily ever after beginning at age twenty-seven."[57] Or maybe that's just me, but you know what I mean.

We all have a general plan based in some type of expectation. We expect to get the job we want. We expect to pass our exams on the first try. We expect to be married with kids before thirty. We expect to get the promotion we've been working towards. And we expect to receive those things *when* we expect to receive them. If we don't, we get down in the dumps while we wait.

I hear a lot of people say some variation of "God's no just means not yet." Sometimes that's true and our answer truly is "not yet." Sometimes we are in a season of waiting for the moment God declares, "Now is your turn." Sometimes He needs to prepare our hearts or minds or bodies before He says, "Yes."

But y'all, sometimes "no" just means no. Sometimes the very thing you want or believe will make you better or somehow "more" is the thing God loves you too much to give you. Because He knows the truth. He knows the thing you want so desperately—the husband you don't have, the baby you can't conceive, the corner office, the job at XYZ Company—may be for your good, but it's not for your best. It doesn't fit in His plan for you. It might even hinder the plan He has designed with you in mind. He knows every day of your life, past, present, and future, because He is sovereign and has an eternal perspective. Sometimes God's "no" really does mean no.

When that is the case, know His answer is given with His higher perspective, seeing the future "yes" He will give you that allows you to embrace the abundant life, the full life He craves to give you. We need to be prepared to lay down those dreams of ours at the foot of the cross so we can pick up the plans He has for us. They may not be extravagant in our current perspective, but man oh man, they are better. They are best.

As I found myself preparing to start my new job, I couldn't help but be shocked at how unexpected this was. I enjoyed the work I accomplished in my previous position. I liked the people I worked with (even when they drove me slightly crazy), and I was good at what I did. Then God, in all of His Sovereign power, opened a door I thought had been shut and locked tight. How did this happen? I don't really know other than God made it happen. What I do know is just as He equips us to do the work He is calling us to, He prepares our hearts to be ready when the call comes.

Before this job offer even came along, I began having these moments at my now-former job of "Is this really what I'm supposed to do?"

and "Is this really where I'm supposed to be?" and then, "Why am I thinking this? I've only been here for two years!" These questions were floating around in my mind, and I'm only now beginning to recognize these questions as the Lord preparing my heart for a career move I had not intended to make. Even though I didn't see it at the time, it was as if He began to feed these questions to me, and my response was to ask them back.

With all these questions swirling around, I began praying for guidance, asking that He would open a door if that was not where I needed to be anymore, and asking for courage to walk through whichever door He might open. And my goodness, did He open a door. It was not at all the door I expected (remember, I thought this particular door was locked for good), but the Lord revealed Himself again to me as the Lord of my planner.

My door came in the form of one email, sent from the Controller of the company who I had worked with as an intern four years before, asking me to consider taking a job that had become available. After setting up a phone call a few days later, I couldn't help but ask her why she had thought of reaching out after we hadn't really spoken for more than two or three years. Slightly puzzled, she just said, "Well, we have talked to a few other candidates, but your name just kept coming to mind and so I knew I had to reach out."

Tell me that wasn't the Lord. Tell me that wasn't a nudge from the Holy Spirit in both of our hearts, preparing her to reach out and preparing me to take the offer. As if this was icing on the cake, did I mention the email came on the day of the biggest tax deadline? The day that signified I was done with tax season and free to move on to something new, should something new come open.

Even now, I get chills at how good our Father is. He is the God Who knows exactly where I need to go and exactly where I need to be and exactly when I need to be there. He is the God Who will move mountains or the heart of a Controller to help me get there, and He is ready to do the same for you.

I don't want to make it seem like this transition was easy, because it wasn't. This new job was surprising and it was exciting, but it was still a new job. I had to decide whether or not to take it. I had to have hard conversations with my previous employer as I explained why I was leaving. I had to choose to accept a position that felt as if it was turning my entire career plan upside down, and honestly I still haven't quite figured out what my career plan looks like with this new job. Even so, I had prayed for an open door and seeing the Lord open this door in a way only He could, I knew He would fill me with courage to step into this new thing.

Sometimes I'm guilty of thinking the Lord has led me to Point A so He probably wants me to stay here for about five years, and then He'll tell me to move to somewhere else *(location TBD)*. On the other hand, I sometimes think I'll be at Point A for as long as the Lord tells me to be here, and then He will tell me to move to the Point B I've already decided myself *(timeline TBD)*.

In both scenarios, I am guilty of trying to heap my expectations upon the Sovereign Lord. I have to remind myself He is in control of both place *and* time. He has never been nor ever will be wrong on either count. I, however, have been wrong on both. This is why we can trust in the promises He has spoken over each of us.

In both the waiting for what we want and accepting what we never intended to hold, we must not forget the faithfulness of the Lord in the lives of every believer who came before us and His continuing promise to be faithful in our lives. God's promises are much more secure than our personal expectations. As we wait, the longer we wait, the more we lean into His promises of perfect timing and abundant life, the sweeter His promises sound when the wait is over.

Abraham didn't expect God to lead him out of the land of his ancestors to live as a foreigner for the rest of his life, and he later didn't expect he would be asked to sacrifice the very son he had waited for until he was one hundred years old and who God had given him to fulfill His covenant promise. Moses didn't expect the Promised Land to be forty years in the distance, just as He didn't expect God's plan was for Him to lead the people there. Joshua wouldn't have expected the walls of Jericho to fall after seven days of walking around them just as he wouldn't have expected trumpet sounds and a loud shout to be enough to make the walls fall had God not told him beforehand.

These men made it into the Hebrews "Hall of Fame" because they trusted God's plan *and* God's timing. They were willing to abandon the life they had dreamt up for themselves because they had faith in the superior plans of God. I love what the author of Hebrews says in chapter 11, verses 8-9 (NLT):

> *"It was by faith that Abraham obeyed when God called him to leave home and go to another land that God would give him as his inheritance. He went without knowing where he was going. And even when he had reached the land God promised to him, he lived there by faith…"*

He went without knowing where he was going. This is the faith I want for myself and for you. When God calls us to go, we go, even when we don't know where we are going. And when we get there, when we reach the place God has promised to bring us to, we live there by faith. We don't just need faith in the waiting and in the journey; we need faith when we reach our destination. When we enter the sacred space of God's unique plan for us, both place and time, we stay by faith.

Y'all, God has all of this figured out. He knows exactly how my career is going to pan out, even though I don't even know what the next year is going to look like. Just as He knew Sarah would give birth to Isaac when Abraham was one hundred years old, just as He knew Moses would wander in the desert for forty years, and just as He knew the walls of Jericho would fall after seven days, He knows the timetable for our lives.

Time and time again, He has revealed Himself as worthy of every ounce of faith we can muster. He might meet the expectations we have, but more likely, He will exceed our expectations. Yes, it might take longer than our expected time frame. Yes, it might look extremely different than the plan we made for ourselves. Yes, it might seem to happen all at once and we might even feel overwhelmed at how quickly our lives are changing. But this is what God does. He is the Lord of our planner, the Keeper of our "best." He knows the plans we've made for ourselves. He knows the time frame in which we want things to happen. He also knows His plans are far better, far greater to serve His purposes, for our good and His glory when they happen on His timeline.

Please, don't put a cap on the goodness in which He wants you to live. Expect Him to do exceedingly and abundantly more than you can ask or think.[58] Why? Because He can and He will. The question isn't whether or not He can work in your life; the question is: will you be looking for Him as He works?

If you find yourself reading this in a time of waiting, I hope you can begin to let go of the grip you have on what you think your life should look like and instead, hold tight to the promises of God Who loves you enough to plan a life for you before a single day had come to pass.[59] Letting go of expectations is not easy and it's definitely not comfortable, but God knows this. He knows it might be difficult for you to release the plan you've held in your heart and mind for years. He gives you enough grace to work through the process of untying all those strings you've wound together so deeply in your heart and laying that freshly cleared space before Him to fill with the work He's created you to do. If you allow God to help you through this process and allow the Holy Spirit to work in your heart, creating expectations not of what you want but what He wants for you, He has promised to see you through.

He will guide you where you need to be. Maybe it will be to the job you've wanted for so long, but maybe it will be to another career field altogether. Maybe it will be the man He has chosen to be your spouse, but maybe He is calling you to first accomplish something for His Kingdom that does not include a spouse...maybe His plans don't include a spouse at all. Maybe He will lead you back home to the place you were raised, but maybe His plans are for you to influence and encourage a new community to find their place in the family of the Most High God. And maybe He will lead you to write while sitting on your childhood porch on a warm summer day with the family pets sitting next to you.

The point is, there are no limits to what the Lord can do if we only relinquish our lives and our plans and our expectations to Him. He is the only one who will never disappoint. So even in the waiting, praise Him for working. Praise Him for knowing what you need more than you do. Praise Him for loving you too much to open a door that isn't the best option. Praise Him for being with you in the silence.

And to the ones who may have just came out of a season of waiting, I hope you (like I'm trying to do myself at the moment) take time to celebrate what the Lord has just done in your life. This new step may be a stop along the way to prepare you for something bigger the Lord is working in your life, or it may be the answer to a prayer you've been praying for many years. Either way, He has called your number, or more correctly, He has called you by your name, and it is your turn. So praise Him for the move. Praise Him for the answer. Praise Him for the job. Praise Him for the ability to stay home with your new baby. Praise Him for the first date that may or may not lead to marriage. Praise Him. The Lord of your planner is here.

AS YOU GROW UP: A LETTER FROM LATONYA HOCKETT

I remember saying when I started dating my now-husband that I wanted to be married at twenty-five and pregnant at twenty-seven. I wanted three kids and I had my life all planned out in that particular area. Well, I came to understand what the scripture in Proverbs 16:9 says in the NLT that "we can make our plans, but the Lord determines our steps." Only part of the plan I had stated has come to fruition. I got married at twenty-eight and at the age of forty-one, I am still waiting and believing for children. Waiting has definitely been teaching me faith and patience, as well as beloved identity. The important thing to know about waiting is that it is only for a season. It doesn't last forever, even though it may feel like forever.

My husband and I have been waiting for over ten years for babies. We have gone through the tests, surgeries, procedures, etc. Through it all, I have continued to believe that, in God's timing, our babies will become a reality for us. As I continue my journey of waiting, treasures from Heaven have helped me to maintain a posture of faith in God. In November of 2016, the Lord gave me an acronym for WAIT, When Abba Interprets Time. His timing could be one year, ten years, or one month from now. Keep trusting and keep believing. He is a man of His word.

What I wish I'd known when I first started this journey of waiting was that waiting isn't a curse, and it doesn't mean you've done something wrong. I wish I had known how important it is to experience the sadness, madness, and anger of waiting as well as the beauty of waiting. Waiting should empower you. Waiting brings revelation of who God is in your life. Waiting floods your life with hope. Lamentations 3:25-26, NIV, says, "The Lord is good to those whose hope is in Him, to the ones who seek Him; it is good to wait quietly for the salvation of the Lord." I wish I had known that in the waiting, a beautiful journey begins. It's time where intimacy grows with the

Father. Waiting is a place where it's only you and Him. You can be yourself and grow to love yourself as He reveals. The beauty of waiting creates this wonderful blooming effect in your own personal garden. Waiting does not diminish you; waiting disciplines you and teaches you. I wish I could have seen how special it was to be considered to wait on the Lord for such a time as this. This time in my life is not about me. It's about bringing glory to Abba. It's about testifying of the goodness of waiting well. It's being an example to others of what it looks like to trust in the Lord with all your heart and lean not on your own understanding. Waiting in God transcends time. Will you allow Abba to interpret time for YOU?

I pray as you're maturing in life you would remember this: God knows what's best for you. He knows when to bring those promises into your life. Never think lower than yourself when you find you have to wait on the Lord concerning anything in your life. He created you. He carved out your journey just for you! There are things only YOU can do. So when you find yourself anxious or doubting in the waiting, ask yourself, "What lesson should I be learning in this moment? How can I be of service to others?"

I found myself seeking the Lord in prayer, reading and meditating to help me in those times of anxiety and doubt. I also found other things I am passionate about while I'm waiting. So, remember to not waste your wait. There are plenty of treasures to be found while you're in this season. Make the most of it. I'm grateful I've learned to be thankful during this time. I am enjoying my husband, I'm enjoying the quiet of my house during this pandemic, with no children. I can pick up and go without having to call a babysitter right now! So, there are some positives to this thing called wait! I pray you understand there are hills and valleys on everyone's journey. Allow yourself to sit in the good as well as the not-so-good times of waiting. They will both bring you to a good place as you learn to trust in God and grow deeper in His love for you. I encourage you to allow the Lord to be your planner.

CHAPTER 11
Freedom of Dependence

Has anyone ever told you that you were in control? That you are the only one who can make things happen for yourself and, oh by the way, your life and your happiness depend on you? You are the captain of your own ship and you get to decide where you sail! You are your own hero, so go out there and kick some booty and take names, because you can do whatever you want, go wherever you want, reach as high as you want, and be as successful as you want!

If you are nodding your head and throwing a fist in the air because hearing these things make you want to go out and change the world… this might not be the book for you. Or maybe this is exactly the book for you because hopping on the "you can do it on your own" train is a trap so many of us are falling into right now. There, I said it. It's a trap. If you don't identify as a believer of Jesus Christ, then by all means, you do you. Go out there and do your thing because even if you don't believe in power of God, He can use your ambition to further His purposes in this world. But if you believe in the Word of God and the reconciliation story of Jesus Christ dying for us, I will beg as persistently as the woman to the judge in Luke 18 for you to hear this:

You are not in control.

Every time I hear someone try to tell me I am in control of my own life, my heart does a deep dive into the pit of my stomach. As someone who fought for years to "maintain control" of my life only to be hit by a train in a moment with something feeling a lot like a loss of control permeating every part of my life, I have learned. Re-learned, and re-re-learned the lesson of the Proverbs:

"In their hearts humans plan their course, but the Lord establishes their steps."[60]

"Many are the plans in a person's heart, but it is the Lord's purpose that prevails."[61]

These are both verses I have heard many times over, and until recently, I tended to skip over the first half of each verse.

"In their hearts humans plan their course."

"Many are the plans in a person's heart."

It's interesting to me how both of these verses echo the fact that plans dwell in our hearts. We have hopes and dreams and plans and desires in our hearts. There's no use denying it with the churchy saying "God's plan is my plan" or something similar but equally off-putting to anyone who hasn't allowed the Lord to lead them. We have our own plans. We all know where we want to go in life, what we want to do, and with whom we want to do it.

It's in our nature to plan. We live with goals in mind because they give us something to work toward. I recently had to set new goals for my next year of work: five goals I plan to accomplish by the end of our fiscal year. This is a practice I've done in every year of work, and it is present in some form in every business. I actually really love setting goals. I love writing my goals out and planning how I'm going to make them happen. It's how I operate. I like to know why I'm doing what I'm doing and where I'm trying to go. If you are a fellow planner, first know you are my soul sister and I understand the desire to plan out every detail so you know what to expect.

I've said before that the Lord has been teaching me He is the Lord of my planner, but I want to dive a little deeper into the planning process. He knows what my plans are, He knows what His plans are for me, and He sees the disparity between the two and how it's all going to fit together to accomplish His purpose. God knows I like to plan because He built that desire into my heart and He doesn't build bad things. Plus, He is a planner Himself.

Our God builds up people, generation after generation, to partner with Him in accomplishing His plans. From the beginning of creation, He had a plan established for reconciling us to Himself by the sacrifice of Jesus. Through the lives of Abraham, Jacob, Ruth, David, and many other men and women, He was planning for the coming of Jesus, working all things together even thousands of years before that first Christmas night.

This chapter is not meant to deter you from planning a life for yourself. I absolutely recognize the Lord as being in control of my path, but this acknowledgment doesn't mean I stop planning. We aren't told to just sit back, not do anything at all, and just let the Lord do His thing, although if that's the way He wanted to work, then we better pull up a chair and watch what happens because He does not need us to make things happen. The Lord doesn't tell us to stop planning in these verses, although that's what I've believed for many years now. It's almost as if these verses are the Lord's way of saying, "Hey, I know you have plans and that's okay, but if your plans are different than mine, be prepared for your plans to change."

We're told to guard our hearts,[62] the dwelling place of plans and dreams, above all else. Why? Because while the plans and goals taking up residence in our heart are not bad in themselves, our sinful nature can quickly distort our heart's desires and turned them into control issues when we forget the last half of these verses. Y'all, planning is not the problem; control is.

"...but the Lord establishes their steps."

"...but it is the Lord's purpose that prevails."

I once heard a woman speaking on the Neuroscience of Relationships at a leadership retreat for the nonprofit I'm involved in, and during her presentation she made a comment about how when you read or hear the word "but" in a sentence, that one word negates everything you said before it. (Please don't go back and count how many times I've used that word in this book.) When we look again at these two Proverbs and apply this science, we see the Lord has veto power over our plans. We can make plans, but the Lord establishes our steps. We can dream dreams, but the Lord's purpose prevails. Our plans and dreams may be good, but if they are not aligned with the work the Lord has already laid out for us to do, He has the power to overrule us to accomplish His purposes.

This is something I have struggled with for as long as I can remember. I have a plan and if things don't go as I expect, I find myself in a whirlwind of anxiety. If I can't control the outcome, I feel panicked, uncertain of myself and what's happening around me. If I plan to be a successful business woman by age thirty and don't quite accomplish the feat, I will feel like a failure who single-handedly ruined my own life. If I'm at work and a project I'm leading goes sideways, I feel like it's all my fault. If I don't know where I'm going next, if I can't see the next step, I can freak out faster than you can parody the "Simma Down Now" SNL skit.[63]

I've always had an independent streak in me, and this desire for independence is actually a desire to do things *my* way, a desire for control. I couldn't wait to turn sixteen so I could drive myself all over town and not have to rely on anyone to get me places. For the first twenty-two years of my life, I lived like I was in the driver's seat. I had my plans, my goals, and my lead foot I wouldn't let off the gas long enough to let someone help me along. In relationships, if I ever felt like I was starting to rely on someone else or if I found myself leaning on any one person for support, I wished for an eject button like the one in *2 Fast 2 Furious* where Roman Pearce shouts "Ejecto seato cuz" before pressing a button that literally throws a guy out of the car.[64]

I do not like needing help. I don't like not being able to do something on my own. I don't like having to trust someone will help me, because I worry they won't actually come through (because you for sure can't control anyone else, you know). I doubt others would be willing to help, so I don't bother asking. I fear being let down, so I do things on my own because I couldn't let myself down. I thought needing help, relying on other people, revealing my struggles, and crying in front of other people were signs of weakness. Feeling what I was feeling felt wrong, and so I worked so hard to control everything, my emotions, my plans, my life, my career.

When I entered the workplace, this independence taught me to attempt problems on my own, but my independence was also the roadblock to working well on a team. Having solid problem-solving skills is useful in my job but forgoing opportunities to work with people because I'm not convinced of their ability to get the job done at the level I deem acceptable is not only harmful to my personal growth but also damaging to those I have wrongly judged as incapable.

I know this sounds awful, but this is how I operated and it breaks my own heart because I see how wrong this thought process is. Not only is it not true, it's exhausting to live out. It's exhausting to live and strive in the mindset of "I can do this because I am in control and I want to be happy so this is what I have to do." It's not sustainable.

Being in control means never knowing rest. Being (or fighting to be) in control means constant striving to stay in control because life is constantly moving and shifting and changing, bringing with it new challenges and unforeseen and unplanned struggles. As much as I like to think otherwise, we cannot keep up.

Knowing that striving for control and avoiding help was not the healthiest way to live, the Lord started placing people in my life I could rely on, that I could lean on. People who made me feel safe and would become the hands and feet of Jesus when all my walls started crumbling down. I've sprinkled pieces of the most difficult part of my story in every chapter, and this one is no different.

During my blessed fiasco of 2018, I truly believe the Lord was breaking me of my independence. My entire life had been "Don't let people see the pain you feel. Don't let people know when you're not happy. Don't let people into your struggle. You can handle this all on on your own." But y'all when you can't even get out of a bed by yourself, you learn a little something about the value of dependence. Any semblance of control and any independence I once felt were absolutely shattered with every beat of my heart and left in their places was a desperate need to depend on God and allow the people He so carefully placed in my life to help me.

It was through this period of my life I learned the truth in A.W. Tozer's words: "God being Who and What He is, and we being who and what we are, the only thinkable relation between us is one of full lordship on His part and complete submission on ours."[65] Complete submission. These two words have made me want to run for the hills for as long as I can remember. I'm not going to get into the debate of husbands and wives, but I am going to plead with you to recognize the importance of complete submission to the Lord. John 5 says this:

> *Jesus replied, "Truly I tell you, the Son is not able to do anything on his own, but only what he sees the Father doing. For whatever the Father does, the Son likewise does these things...I do not seek my own will, but the will of him who sent me."[66]*

Jesus, the Son of God, the Savior of the world, the perfecter of our faith, lived by complete submission to the Father. Why do we work so hard for control when Jesus Himself didn't? Why do we strive and hustle and burn ourselves out trying to be everything to everyone when Jesus Himself laid down His life in submission to the Father?

My experience may seem like a really dramatic way to get across the point of us not being in control, but this is what it took for me to learn that lesson. My hope is you won't have to learn this lesson the hard way. I hope you will recognize the lordship of God and submit to His plan, His will, His way, His when, His how, and His why.

He deserves no less than every ounce of our dependence. Whether at work or at home or at the altar or anywhere in between. The Lord makes it extremely clear our job is not to be the captain of our own ship. The Lord makes it extremely clear that if we, as children of God and followers of Jesus Christ, start creating the life we want outside of His will, He has the power to redirect us. His purpose will prevail every day of the week.

Beyond that, Paul says this in 2 Corinthians:

> *"Each time he said: 'My grace is all you need. My power works best in weakness.' So now I am glad to boast about my weaknesses so that the power of Christ can work through me…for when I am weak, then I am strong."*[67]

For twenty-two years of my life, I saw needing help as being weak. As the Lord broke me until I had no choice but to seek help, He reminded me of these words. Independence does not equate to strength. Being in control does not mean we are strong. Inviting people into our journey, asking people to walk with us, asking people to support us and encourage us and help us—this is where our strength lies. When we recognize our weakness and our inability to make it through this life on our own, the power of Christ can rest upon us. He can bring us strength in the form of people standing beside us in the fight and His own power working through us.

This doesn't mean we are free-loaders, coasting through every day with no care in the world and no responsibility to our name. Allowing God to reign in your life, giving in to the absolute authority He already has, letting God have His way with your life and in your heart, this is where we truly begin to live. This is where we find freedom to live the life He has already established for us, and may we not forget with freedom comes responsibility. Not control, but responsibility. Responsibility to steward the gifts He has given you well. Responsibility to chase the dreams and goals He has placed in your heart. Responsibility to choose Him and choose His path for you every day you open your eyes to a new day.

I don't know about you but just reading these words releases the pressure of being in control and replaces the pressure with peace. We are not in control. I am not in control. By the grace of God, we are given free will to make our own choices. When we make the choice to follow His leading, our choices become a reflection of what He wants for us because we start looking for His will, His direction, His wisdom in choosing to go right or go left. In her book, *A Woman After God's Own Heart,* Elizabeth George echoes this sentiment in saying, "God wants my heart—all of it— and my devotion. When I choose to give it to Him, when I choose to live totally for Him, He makes it count." [68]

Handing over control is something I still struggle with. It's the reason I very much feel like having a panic attack when I have to board an airplane. It's the reason I insist on driving on 95% of all the trips I take. It's the reason I plan for my future. At this moment, I am sitting on an airplane 39,000 feet in the air...alone. I'm surrounded by people, but I am flying alone and it scares the daylights out of me because I'm not in control. I have no control over where the pilot is flying. He could be taking us to Newark instead of Nashville for all I know, and there's nothing I could do about it. The difference is I now recognize the futility in trying to control what happens. I recognize the Sovereignty of the Lord and my absolute dependence on Him to calm my fears, save me of my anxious thoughts, and lead me along the path He has set before me.

I need God. I need His presence, His stillness, and His strength. I need to know He is in control because then I can rest in His everlasting arms. It's only when I give up the notion of control that I am released from the exhaustion of trying to figure everything out on my own. I'm not on my own, and neither are you. God is with us, Immanuel. Prince of Peace. Lord of planners. Keeper of control.

So in recognizing the lordship of God in our lives, how do we plan? What does it look like to make a plan for our future and live in complete dependence upon the Lord to meet our every need? I think this is a tough balance to find, because it is hard to have plans and to work toward something but also recognize you can be overruled and detoured to something new. It's hard to pour energy and time and resources into something and then have it fade away into the land of unattained dreams. It's hard to have a plan when it could change at any moment.

As tough as it is, it is absolutely worth it. It is so special to look at plans you've made and compare them to the prevailing purpose of God. Go to Scripture. Dig into the words of the Master Planner in the hopes that if the plans you've dreamt on your own are not in line with His, He will begin to shift your heart. Philippians 2:13 (NLT) says "For God is working in you, giving you the desire and the power to do what pleases him." When we find ourselves faced with a change of plans or a shifting of our heart towards something unexpected, I hope we would remember these words of Paul to the Christians in Philippi. God is working in you. As you relinquish control to the Almighty God, He will shift your heart and your desires to align with His own. Then, as His grand plan begins to unfold in your life, He will give you the power to do what pleases Him.

- We seek His will in all we do, depending on Him, not our own understanding to show us which path to take.[69]

- We plan our actions, but we commit those actions to the Lord.[70]

- We believe in the beauty of His timing, even though we cannot see the whole scope of God's work from beginning to end.[71]

- We keep on asking for the Lord to lead us, we keep on seeking His presence as we step into new things, we keep on knocking on the doors we find, trusting that He will open the one that is intended for us.[72]

Beyond our need for control, beyond our desire for a corner office or a business with our name on the sign, beyond our hopes for the perfect husband and cutest children, we are followers of Christ. We may be leaders in our field or our community, but we are followers first. We follow the leading of the Sovereign God, Who rejoices in our decision to give up our perception of control and choose to be reliant upon Him.

In His rejoicing, He pours out His favor in our lives. He opens the doors that couldn't be opened until He knew you would stand at the open door, until He said to walk through it (remember Noah and the Ark?).[73] He gives you the honor and privilege of being called a child of God and a co-heir with Christ. He gives you saving grace and mercy that is more than the mistakes of your past and your future. He leads you along the life He specifically and intentionally designed for you. He fills you with His Holy Spirit which allows you to experience His peace and His rest, even in the chaos of this ever-changing life. It is only by giving up the fight for control that we can pick up the true call on our lives.

AS YOU GROW UP: A LETTER FROM D. MICHELLE THOMPSON

I remember when I first felt the Lord prompting me to marketplace ministry full-time to be free and independent as an entrepreneur. I thought I was truly submitted to depending upon God for provision and not the security of a full-time check from a Fortune 100 company. I couldn't wait to publish my first book, written in my late twenties and then published in my late thirties. I eagerly embraced it like a shiny new white canvas…I plotted a six-month plan prior to resigning from my job and going on a book tour. In the final month of the plan, I ordered 3,000 copies of my book to ensure going beyond the industry statistic that most independent authors don't sell more than 3,000 copies their first year. Within two or three months, I had a guaranteed speaking engagement at a worldwide ministry and a call to distribute my book as a TV talk show.

I thought surely this was my reward for being "truly" dependent upon God. I sold my car, I signed a contract with a real estate agent to sell my condo. I even broke a family commitment to pay off a debt, all because I truly thought I was forsaking all else for the Lord to be at work on purpose. Yet, I ended up selling the car well below value because I saw a veteran in need, I ended up after a year and several refinances losing my home versus selling it and the debt I paused merely returned to making payments for surely I owe nothing but to love. Oh and the 3,000 books had so many typos I had to reorder and the TV network that wanted to distribute my talk show based off my book completely folded and I helped them move the furniture out of their offices to a storage space.

While I embraced the shiny white canvas as dependence on God, I didn't submit or surrender to the proper roles in creating the master-piece. You probably see it more clearly from the outside looking in, but I was so close to it, I didn't see the Creator, the One who spoke and everything was, who breathed life into man, who is omnipresent and omniscient, is the great artist and I a mere white canvas.

Why did I miss it? I, like many of us, was so busy planning what I wanted it to look like I didn't see the canvas was becoming two different paths, yet in His grace, He would always lead me to the singular end…at home with Him, knowing I belong to Christ. This belief gives me the freedom (not excuse), to not plan, but to hold it with an open hand, to just focus on being the canvas ready to soak in whatever color the Savior has for me trusting the ultimate design is His destiny for my life, a workmanship, a masterpiece created for His glory!

So I pray you would remember as you're growing up that You Belong to Christ! It is because of this dependent positioning, belonging to Christ, you can always be joyful, pray without ceasing and continue to be thankful in every situation, even the difficult ones described in this chapter.

Growing Up between the Office and the Altar, I encourage you on a daily basis to choose:

1. To surrender to His will and not your own. Promotion is from the Lord, trust Him to promote in the season it is for you to be promoted or transition into a different career path.

2. To see that sacrifice is not a planned event, but a response to Holy Spirit promptings. Tithes and offerings are a blessing, but what does it look like for a daily sacrifice not to "fit" in to reflect who you belong to in the workplace. (e.g. No, it's not a sign on your desk but an act of the heart)

3. To seek God through His Word and in quiet times of reflected prayer. Remember you are His temple and the altar goes where you go. Remember to take your break times to reflect on His Word or invite His Holy Spirit to lead you at work as He is the artist and there is a piece to the masterpiece at work.

CHAPTER 12

One Body

Raise your hand if you hated group projects in school!

You can't see my hands right now but rest assured, they are both lifted high like goal posts, because to say I was not a fan is an understatement. I seemed to be the one everything fell onto, the one who did the whole project, including writing the other members' names at the top of the document. Part of the problem was teachers always seemed to put me in a group of less dedicated members, but the other part of the problem was the expectations I had for myself and my group were almost always higher than everyone else's. They wanted to get it over with; I wanted to have the best project in the class. Call it an Enneagram Type 1 hazard but those high (aka-perfect) expectations resulted in me doing all the work.

I was so excited to graduate and start my career off with a bang, group projects be gone! I hate to break the news if you haven't figured it out already, but group projects don't end after school. Teamwork is a hallmark of almost every field of work. The success of most work projects are attributed to the team of co-workers who come together to accomplish a single task. Synergy is what we're after here, people!

Employers promote team-building, even when your job is to prepare a tax return. You may think this is a pretty solitary job, but it requires much more communication and teamwork than I ever anticipated. I didn't expect to keep working in groups past college, and I certainly didn't expect to enjoy it, but I did. My first years of full-time work would have looked a lot different, a lot more lonely, and would have been severely lacking in personal and professional growth had it not been for the amount of time I spent building relationships and co-laboring with coworkers. Hardly a day went by that one of us didn't shout over our cubicle walls for help or walk over to another office and ask to talk through a particularly difficult problem. My coworkers challenged me. They pushed me to keep learning, to do my part, to speak up when something didn't add up, and to challenge them all the same.

Y'all, the community of believers around us are there for the very same purpose. Our community is meant to push us toward learning more about Jesus, to do our part in serving right where we are (and maybe around the world too), to be accountable to and for each other, and above all, to share Jesus.

It doesn't seem right to think about teamwork and community without first diving into Ephesians 4 and 1 Corinthians 12. As much as I would love to copy these chapters in their entirety, I will simply copy a few verses here and urge you to go back and read the entire chapters on your own.

> *"For there is one body and one Spirit, just as you have been called to one glorious hope for the future. There is one Lord, one faith, one baptism, one God and Father of all, who is over all, in all, and living through all. However, he has given each one of us a special gift through the generosity of Christ...He makes the whole body fit together perfectly. As each part does its own special work, it helps the other parts grow, so that the whole body is healthy and growing and full of love."[74]*

"If one part suffers, all the parts suffer with it, and if one part is honored, all the parts are glad. All of you together are Christ's body, and each of you is a part of it."[75]

We need community. We rejoice, we grieve, we cry (when the tears are happy and sad), we dig through trenches, we walk through the beautiful design of life as written and produced by the one true God, and we need to do it all together. We were designed to be the body of Christ, one single body of millions of people uniquely equipped with a *special gift through the generosity of Christ*. We were designed to work in teams. We were made for this.

My problem with group projects in college was my expectations of how things should be done were vastly different from those of my group members. I wanted to be the best, and so they needed to step up and do things exactly how I wanted them done because I had already decided what "best" looked like. Starting out in my career, I couldn't even pretend to know best. Well I could, but that didn't get me very far. After a few weeks of thinking I knew best, I quickly learned I needed to rely on other people with more experience and a clearer understanding of what we needed to do to be the best. I needed to do my part, my job, and trust my coworkers would do theirs, too, so that together, we could meet our collective goals.

I think the same is true for our work in the Body of Christ. We could walk in to the pastor's office on Sunday and say, "Okay, I have it all figured out. Here's the plan for what we need to do to be the best and bring everyone to Jesus." Want to guess how that would turn out? The truth is, the best thing we can do in the body of Christ is the work the Lord created for us to do and trust He will bring the right people into play to accomplish His bigger purpose.

Sometimes it's overwhelming to look at all the work that needs to be done in the world. It's overwhelming to look around at all the people who are grieving the loss of a parent, a friend, a spouse, a baby. It's overwhelming to see the evil that could take innocent children and turn them into slaves. It's overwhelming to hear of shootings and bombings and wars which seem to be unending. It's overwhelming to see a generation— to be part of a generation— that is growing up with a fear in our hearts for the very real threat of being propositioned at work or attacked in a parking lot after walking out of a grocery store or drugged at a bar. All of it is just too much to hold. I don't know why these things happen, and to be honest, I don't think we'll get an answer other than to know we live in a broken and corrupted world.

This is why we need each other. This is why we need a group of people around us to do life with. We need people to speak truth into our lives, we need people who remind us of Jesus and His faithful promises, we need people who tell us again and again that "perfect love casts out fear"[76] and that perfect love comes in the form of an ever-present God. We need these people, and we need to be these people. We were never meant to do it all on our own.

One morning as I sat down to read part of Francis Chan's *Letters to the Church,* a woman at Starbucks approached me to ask what the book was about. As we began to discuss the differences between the Church as designed in the Bible and the Church we experience today, she told me of her father who had been a deacon at a church in Memphis, Tennessee, for many years until he began having symptoms of dementia which forced a move to Nashville.

She talked about her father's commitment to his church and how he was hesitant to abandon them, even with the distance that now stood between them, so he maintained his relationships as best he could. She then told me his church recently called to say they were bringing "a van full of people" from three hours away to see one of their long-time leaders and fellow brother-in-Christ the next week.

As she was speaking, I couldn't help but think that this was such a

beautiful example of how we are called to live. A body of believers
sacrificing their personal time for a few hours of fellowship with
a brother who may not even recognize them at this point. These
people knew their call and they were answering that call well.

A few months ago, my church started going through a transition
period. The emotions in the air on that first Sunday after the
announcement that our lead pastor was leaving were evident, even
to someone like me who had only witnessed a few years of his time
at our church. There was sadness, anger, confusion, and a sense
of feeling lost. The sermon was raw with the combination of these
emotions as another one of the pastors preached. Then, at the end
of the sermon, he called all the people to the front of the sanctuary.
All able-bodied men, women, and children crowded the front of the
church, laid hands on one another, and simultaneously lifted our
prayers to the Supreme Christ, the God Who was not surprised by
the events of that week, the God Who already saw the healing and
restoration we joined together to pray for. It was powerful.

Families, friends, and strangers. Young, old, and in between. Male
and female. Stay at home moms, business executives, and pastors. All
brought our emotions to the Lord. In the midst of the emotion, there
was a sense of togetherness, of connection, of oneness as our unique
prayers and emotions were spoken, cried, silently thought, and lifted
up as a united body of believers. Just thinking back to that moment
brings me to tears.

These are just two examples of what community is for. Coming
together, suffering with one another, bringing our real and raw
emotions, dropping the "I'm okay" facade and allowing ourselves
to be vulnerable with our people and with God. Even in the great
sorrow visible on the many faces around me that Sunday and on the
face of the woman at Starbucks, there was praise for the Lord Who
is big enough to handle our sorrow and lead us into restoration and
peace. There was praise for the Son and the redemption He died to

offer us. There were tears of sadness, but there was also gratitude for the One Who *knows* and Who understands.

Our community is also a place for rejoicing. The same unity that shares in struggles rejoices in health, in growth, and in becoming love. I was reminded of this as I opened my home to host a 4word gathering. I was also reminded I need to clean my bathroom more often.

One of my dearest friends, who is full of Jesus and the ability to plan a great event arrived early to help make sure everything was set up. I was running a bit behind and hadn't had time to *properly* clean, so as she walked into the bathroom, she shouted, "Hey, I'm going to pick up a little in here to make it presentable if that's alright!" I was not at all offended she thought the bathroom was not presentable as it was, because let's be honest: it wasn't. She made the bathroom presentable as I scrambled to get the dishes out of the sink before we welcomed people to our event. This may seem like a silly story, but it stuck with me. I couldn't help but appreciate this friend who took the time to help me make my home ready for guests. It's not that I'm thankful for someone cleaning my bathroom, even though that was a nice bonus. I'm thankful for people who walk through life with us when things are neat and tidy and when our lives resemble a town just hit by a twister.

That night at the event, we listened to another friend speak about David and we shared about difficult times in our lives, but we also had the opportunity to share our joys. I remember that was one of the first nights I spoke about this book I had been writing. I was so excited and I was almost bursting with joy as I shared the news and told of my hopes and my dreams for this book and for you, the reader of these words, and for how God would one day use this to bring Himself glory. A few hours earlier I was worried about how dirty my house was, but in that moment, I knew it was all worth it. My heart was soaring as I shared these thoughts with some of the women at the event and felt their excitement rising for me. These women saw my joy and opened themselves up to share in it with me. This night is among my favorite memories for this very reason.

The point is not that we must have clean and presentable restrooms at all times when having guests (although this probably should happen). The point is that we have guests, that we welcome people into our homes and into our lives. That we experience the joy of celebrating a new job or new business a friend is embarking on. That we pray together for the friends walking through the wilderness. That we experience fellowship which will stand the test of time, much like that Memphis church.

God in all of His sovereignty is more than enough to meet your every need. Some things need to be handled between you and God alone. I've had my fair share of struggles that to this day remain between me and the God Who sees my every move and knows my every thought. But there have been times where I needed God's people. There are still times where I need God's people, and they will be there every time because this is what the Body is built for. In the words of Bob Goff, "sometimes when we ask God for an answer He sends us a friend."[77] I have learned over the past year how important this is for me personally, and I pray with all my heart you will learn the same for yourself.

I'm also learning that our commitment to fellowship is not one-sided. We don't pour out our struggles and our joys to other people and call it a day. We flip the conversation to hear of the struggles and joys of others. We step up and pray for our family. We serve those in our community who need help. We walk alongside those who in the past have walked alongside us. We walk alongside those who maybe don't even know our stories. We are no more in need of help than the person sitting beside us at church on Sunday or at work on Monday.

When we make fellowship all about us and what we need, we miss out on some of God's greatest blessings. When we step into someone else's mess, when we follow the Spirit's leading and pray for someone we don't really know or serve people we typically overlook, when we see the Lord working in the lives of those around us, we experience the oneness and the fullness of joy we were meant to share all along.

Do you remember the story of the paralyzed man Jesus healed?[78] If you need a little refresher, the story tells of a paralyzed man and his friends who took him to see Jesus because they had faith that Jesus could heal their friend. They were unable to get to Jesus with the crowds surrounding Him, so they took the man onto the roof, took off some of the tiles, and lowered this paralyzed man straight down in front of Jesus. And what did Jesus say about the audacity that these men had? Seeing their faith, Jesus said to the man, "Young man, your sins are forgiven."[79] He then told the man to "Stand up, pick up your mat, and go home." The story ends with everyone being "gripped with great wonder and awe" and praising God for the amazing things they saw that day.

What if we lived like these friends? What if we did everything in our power to bring healing to our friends, even if that meant climbing onto a roof, tearing part of that roof off the house, and dropping our friend right at the feet of Jesus? I want to be that kind of friend. Jesus didn't just see the faith of the paralyzed man. He saw *their* faith—the faith of the friends—and responded with a miracle only the Son of God could bring about. If these friends had seen the crowds and decided it wasn't worth their time to get their friend to Jesus, if they saw the crowds and abandoned their friend at the thought of the thousands of other items on their to-do list or the overtime they needed to work that weekend, every person in that house would have missed a miracle.

How many miracles have we missed because of our lack of commitment to our friends, our church, and our communities?

Fellowship is not restricted to the walls of your church. Serving is not restricted to your closest friends. There are many ways to serve, to invest, to commit to a community of believers who will partner with you and allow you to partner with them. There is one body, one Spirit, one glorious hope, and through our many acts of fellowship and service, may we remember no person is exempt from the love of Christ and the promise of eternal life.

Y'all, we were never meant to go through life alone. Just as we were made for a relationship with our Father, we were made for relationship with our brothers and sisters in Christ. As you step into the workplace or whatever the equivalent of that is for you, as you step into your new season, don't close yourself off to community. If you find yourself in a new city, find a body of believers you can plug into and grow with. Find a group of people you can be vulnerable with, that you can welcome into your home and your life even when your bathroom isn't clean. I cannot stress this enough. Work is hard. You may be working in your dream job, but dream jobs aren't always a good dream. You can love your work and still be drowning in darkness. You can love the people you work with and still feel alone. You can love the life you're living, but if you aren't sharing what you have seen and heard the Lord doing in your life with people who can cheer you on in the good and hold you up in the bad you will wake up one day and realize you missed out. Please don't miss out. Don't wait until that day to realize you need fellow believers in your corner.

Please find a community of believers. Find a support group full of people walking through a similar stage of life. I have found great friends and more support and encouragement than I could ever repay in connecting with the young singles group at my church and with the 4word organization, a global ministry specifically designed for women in the workplace.

More than that, don't just find a community. Be part of the community. Commit to suffering, growing, and rejoicing with people. Your office is a fantastic place to share the Gospel and invite people into the body of Christ, but it can also be a source of deep darkness that can wreak havoc on your faith. For this reason, it is crucial to find a place where you are refreshed and renewed in your commitment to Christ and reminded hope cannot be dimmed by the bad lighting of most office cubicles.

At one time or another, each and every one of us will need support. We will need a team and others will need a team that includes us. In love and through an unmeasurable amount of grace and kindness, God brought us near to Him. He gave us a purpose, a good work, and then He made each of our purposes intertwine to fulfill His greater purpose. When we step into the body of believers and commit to being a part of this team, we find the body is filled with the Spirit of God sustaining us in our struggles, rejoicing in our obedience, and empowering us to share the Good News of great joy for all people. One church, one people, one team.

AS YOU GROW UP: A LETTER FROM SUSAN TOLLES

I remember when I became a first-time entrepreneur at fifty-three. With no experience in web design, technology, or publishing, I created a website for women over fifty that instantly took off. I worked long hours with a team of writers sharing lifestyle resources for midlife women, and one of my primary goals was to be in the top five on the first page of Google. After the first year, I realized I didn't even know why I was doing what I was doing, and the information I was sharing became very superficial. As a globally-recognized expert on midlife women and number two on the "women over 50" Google page, I thought, "Is this all there is?"

God was stirring in my heart and I longed to minister to women on a deeper level, to help them overcome their fear and doubt as they looked toward the future. I took another leap of faith and became a certified coach, immersing myself in courses from the top experts in the coaching realm. Over the next two years, I invested way too much money in their programs that were supposed to make me rich and successful. The more I strived for the world's success, the more dissatisfied I became. Was I on the path God had designed for me, or was I following someone else's goals for me? Everyone around me told me I was a shining star, but God was nudging me toward something better.

After a few years running a hard race, I began craving Christian community. I felt alone in a sea of Type-A women who were encouraging me but not praying with me. I longed for authenticity, but all I saw were facades when I attended networking events and seminars. I was following other people's goals, not mine, and no one had given me godly advice to change course. Through a God-designed turn of events, I found 4word, a global community of Christian women in the workplace. I knew I had found what I longed for—real women who genuinely cared about me, not my status.

Five years later, I have journeyed through life with this community of authentic women who love the Lord and put Him above all else. We encourage one another, laugh together, have deep conversations, and most importantly, pray for one another. No one cares about my job title or how much money I make. Everyone cares about my overall wellbeing. It is a community like no other. And the bonus for me came when I stepped into a staff position with 4word and left the stress of pursuing worldly success behind.

So wherever God takes you, I pray you surround yourself with Christian friends, mentors, coaches, and leaders. Follow people who are humble and give God the glory for their achievements. Seek wise counsel when making major decisions, always taking it to the Lord for His validation. Pursue God's plan for your life, not what the world tells you to do. And pray without ceasing. God has more in store for you than you can ever imagine! Just let Him take the lead.

CHAPTER 13
My 91 Cents

We made it, y'all. We made it to the final chapter. Now, I want to share what I call my "ninety-one cents story."

Has anyone ever given you an opinion about something and then followed it up with, "Well that's just my two cents"? Well, this book is what I like to call "My Ninety-One Cents."

Coming out of 2018, you could say I was in a weird place. I was filled with gratitude and more joy than I had ever felt for the God who carried me through that year from pain to recovery to healing, but I was also in a season of spiritual rebuilding. I had been healed, but not yet rebuilt.

Life as I saw it had been broken down to the foundation, and over the next year, new life, new passions, and new directions were rising up in place of old expectations. I spent the last few months of 2018 and all of 2019 sitting with Jesus and letting Him into struggles I had held to myself for so long, recognizing and releasing fears and burdens I hadn't even realized were deeply holding me, and praying that all of this would mean something, somehow. The chapters you've read each signify a new piece of the building, a struggle that has been broken down and rebuilt or is currently under construction.

One of my overarching struggles was reconciling who I was at work to the "new me," the me who now recognized a deep need for Jesus and a desire to bring others to know Him too. The me who could no longer be satisfied with working her life away without connecting faith to work. The workplace is kind of weird, you know? You don't always get to choose who you work with, what your job responsibilities are, what projects you're assigned to, or what kind of desk or office you have. But you do get to choose how you work with people, how well you will try to do your job, how much effort you put into projects, and maybe even how you decorate your desk or office. How could I reconcile all of this back to what Jesus, the Initiator and Perfecter of my faith, would do?

In May of 2019, exactly two days prior to the first anniversary of my surgery, I started to realize what my new role is. I didn't have all the answers, and I still don't, but I started to understand one thing: we have all been invited to partner with Jesus in sharing our stories and spreading the Good News, neither of which involve separating our work from the work of God in us.

In reading my ninety-one cents story, I want you to keep in mind how personally God cares for His children. He knows each of us on an individual level, not only as a group of people He created who won't stay on the straight and narrow path, but as individual people, each wholly loved and chosen for a unique purpose and specific work. The specifics of the work He has for you are different than those of the work He has for me, and He knows your work from mine.

To set the stage: A year before, I had been through seven MRIs in the span of a few weeks in preparation for my surgery. My surgeon and neurologist wanted to make sure they knew what they were getting into beforehand, which I am extremely grateful for, but when the bill came for those scans, it was a hard pill to swallow. Add that to a month of physical therapy three times a week, many office visits to the doctors, and ultimately a brain surgery which cost more than double what my annual salary is (all the praise to Jesus that the insurance company took most of that hit), the financial burden of everything was more than I anticipated. My parents graciously helped out when the burden got a little too heavy for my bank account, but as a new professional on her own in the world, it was hard to accept help even though I didn't have a choice. You could definitely say this was a low point for me in almost every sense of the word.

Now fast forward to that day in May of 2019. After almost a year of my sitting with Jesus and working to build the new life He had been working in me, I found myself back home in Lawrenceburg for the week, in between jobs, lacking a paycheck, and worrying about how I was going to pay my rent without dipping into my savings account (the accountant part of me literally cringed at the thought of this). I found myself sitting in the car with my mother as she grabbed the mail that day, at the house I had not lived in for five years at this point, and imagine my surprise when I saw a piece of mail with my name on it. My mom and I looked at each other with a questioning look as I slipped my finger under the seal to find out what it could possibly be, but we never could have predicted this. In that envelope, sent to my childhood home on a day I just so happened to be in town, was a check. This is where the story gets good, y'all.

This wasn't just any check; this was a reimbursement for overpaying for my MRIs a year before. Want to guess how much this check was for? $749.09. Want to guess how much my upcoming rent payment was? $750.

Y'ALL. That check was within ninety-one cents of the total I had been worried about scrambling together. A year before, I had no idea I was overpaying for my scans and it was physically painful to send that payment, and I certainly had no idea that a year later I would be in between jobs and receive that money back right when I needed it. But God did. He knows. *He knows.* He knows what we need before we need it. He knows how to meet our needs, down to the most basic earthly level.

This is the God we serve. This is the God we can expect to carry us through in ways far greater than we possibly know. I'm amazed. I'm awestruck. I'm just plain overwhelmed at the way God cares for me, for all of us, so intimately. From the timing of the check to the place it was delivered to the check itself…that was a year in the making, He has shown me no detail is beneath Him. No detail of our lives is insignificant or unimportant to Him.

It's these moments, when the Lord reveals Himself in a miraculous way, that we must commit to memory. We see these wonderful displays of the Lord's absolute faithfulness to provide for us, to heal us, to save us, or to sustain us. We experience the joy, His joy, that comes in seeing His work play out before our eyes. We see the beauty being brought out of ashes. We must remember them in every present moment.

In every moment, we are bookended by the Almighty God. On one side, we can look back and see the past faithfulness of God in our lives and the lives of everyone who came before us. On the other side, we can look forward and see the future promises He has given to us and know not one word of His promises will return void. When we put the two together, we find our lives are much like a book being held upright on both sides. Wherever you are, whatever you're doing, you are held in this moment by a God who will not fail on either end. He hems us in behind and before and lays His hand upon us now.[80]

This will be the fuel to keep our eyes fixed on Him, awaiting His next move with joyful expectation, knowing the God we followed yesterday is the God we follow today and will be the God we follow tomorrow. Knowing God is unchanging, we see His past faithfulness and walk with expectation and with confidence that He will continue to provide, heal, save, and sustain. Not only can He do again today what He did yesterday, He can do more.

Now you may be thinking, "That's a pretty cool story but why did you wait to the end to tell it?" Well, y'all, that is a two-part answer. Part one being that I can do that because I'm the writer here. Part two being due in large part to my mentor-turned-friend, Kelli, and her husband Jamey.

After telling Kelli my ninety-one cents story and her relaying it to her husband, I got a call and heard her say, "Jamey wanted me to tell you that you need to figure out what the ninety-one cents mean." Initially, I thought it was pointless because all it meant was that I had to pull ninety-one cents out of my pocket to cover the rest of my rent that month. Then they really got me thinking. What does the ninety-one cents mean? Why did the God of complete intentionality send this check for ninety-one cents less than my rent, when He very easily could have made it the exact amount? After thinking and praying on that, I've landed on this: I think we all have a ninety-one cents story.

Just as He gave me the responsibility of paying ninety-one cents of my rent, He gives me a part to play in His master plan. This book exists because I have been entrusted with a piece of the plan. I have been invited to the party and I want to go. You have been given the same opportunity.

God can do everything all on His own. He doesn't need our help to accomplish His plans. He doesn't need our words and actions to change hearts. He doesn't really even need us at all. But He wants us.[81] He desires to call us His children.[82] He invites us to stand up and walk with Him through this life and the next.[83] He fills us with purpose and asks us to help work those purposes out for His glory.[84]

He calls out our name—my name and your name— and gives us a specific assignment. He carves out ninety-one cents of His master plan, looks our way, and says, "I invite you to be a part of something which matters for eternity." Let me just pump the brakes real quick and tell you to read that again. We aren't forced into it, we aren't begging for a part to play, we don't have to wander down the road aimlessly with no direction and no purpose. We are *invited*. He looks directly at each of us and says, "I want you to accomplish this. I will be here to help you every step of the way, but I want you to work on this for me."

Your "this" could be a job, a service, a mission, a relationship to mend, a conversation to have, a generous gift for someone, an extension of grace, or a family to build. Coming from a creative God, it could literally be anything, but I know He has something for you. He has not forgotten about you. He gives both you and me an invitation to work with Him in this life and live eternally with Him in the next. I don't know about you, but that sounds like the grandest job offer we could ever receive. The question is this: will you accept His offer? Will you commit to living out your ninety-one cents?

AS YOU GROW UP: A LETTER FROM KELLI HENLEY

I remember when I allowed my worth and purpose to be defined by worldly accomplishments and job titles. I wore the number of hours I worked each week like a badge of honor. The office with a window served as proof to myself and everyone else that I had made it. I had made it professionally.

Within the same month of being promoted and receiving a raise from my current employer, God told me, "No." Months earlier, my husband and I received devastating news that his grandfather, who had raised my husband as his son, had six months to live. Suddenly, the hustle and grind of my job seemed completely meaningless. What did how much I worked or how many projects I completed in the next six months matter if I dedicated more time to work than time spent soaking in my last moments with Pa?

God said, "No," because He knew I was made for more. His plan for me is more than working eighty plus hours a week without really working for Him in the midst. All He wanted was more of my time and He used the next six months to literally turn my life upside down. In short, here is a quick list of the ways He moved during that short time period:

- He gave me the courage to leave the place I had worked for over a decade – my first job out of college.

- He pushed me to leave the job title I had dreamed of achieving all of my professional career.

- He delivered an opportunity with a new employer and job title, requiring less hours per week at a higher salary.

- He provided me with more free time and better work/life balance to pursue other passions and dive into His work.

- Both of my husband's grandparents went to be with the Lord on the same day, four hours and forty-five minutes apart.

I am in awe of Courtney's story for reasons of its own; however, I can't shake the overwhelming feeling of parallelism our stories share. Like she, I was stripped of many things: the identity I had formed for myself of Senior Tax Manager at a well-known, established regional accounting firm, the stress and trauma of working long hours for extended time periods, and loved ones. Through the stripping and tearing down comes cleansing and redefining, and eventually, a rebirth of sorts.

What I wish I had known then, heading into 2019, is that God passionately invites us to participate in a relationship with Him. Our only role is to listen. As a self-proclaimed, life-long Christian, I am embarrassed to say that up until this point of my story, I hadn't sat still long enough to listen. Over the last two years of listening, He has created space for people and opportunities in my life which cannot be explained in ways apart from His faithfulness and goodness.

I pray as you're "growing up" you would remember this: listen. Meditate on His word and the relationships and opportunities He has put in your life. His way wants us to marry the ideas of earthly work and Godly work. Through earthly work, He revealed to me that I longed to do His work, meant specifically for me. On the other side, I now know His work for me is to steward women through their health and fitness journeys using Him as our compass. I now know He has intentionally provided me with enough free time to minister to junior high students at my church. I now know I can do His work through building and maintaining meaningful relationships with co-workers in my career as a tax accountant at a healthcare company.

"Whatever you do, work heartily, as for the Lord and not for men."
- Colossians 3:23

EPILOGUE

Do you remember in school when you would be preparing for an exam of some kind and your professor would give you advice for answering the multiple choice questions? The kind where they would give you a question and then lay out options A through D (or more letters, if they were feeling particularly difficult). If your teachers were anything like many of mine, they would say, "Now remember, it's best if you can narrow it down to two answers and then choose from there," or more often, "Remember to stay away from the absolutes. There is almost always an exception to the rule or a special circumstance that makes answers including 'always' or 'never' incorrect." This advice served me well in school and, most importantly, when studying for the dreaded CPA exams (prayers for anyone going through this test or a similar professional exam right now). However, when it comes to the nature and the character of God the Father, Son, and Holy Spirit, the absolutes are everything.

God Himself is unchanging, He is not marked by time or altered by circumstance. While our school teachers and professional bosses lead us away from absolutes, God relishes in their eternal nature. He means what He says, and He invites us to experience the joy and the hope which come when we accept His eternal nature. Words like "always" and "never" and "nothing" and "all" and "everything" bring doubt to our minds when related to things of this world, but when applied to the God of all creation, they are filled with promise.

When thinking of how I wanted to end this book, I didn't want to overwhelm you any more than I maybe already have. I don't want to end this book with words of my own, because at the end of the day, my words are as imperfect as I am. I want the last words to be those of the perfect God who does not change. There are so many more lessons we will learn as we continue to navigate our lives between the altar where we give ourselves over to God and the office where we are working to grow in our careers. There is more life to live and more love to give (and find). Above all, there is God. I pray we would look for Him along our way. I pray we would rejoice in the work He is doing in our lives right in this moment. I pray as we continue growing up in our faith and our careers, we would hold tight to the eternal nature of God and the promises He has given to us. I pray you would read these words over and over again, write them on your heart, repeat them wherever you are and wherever you go.[85] God will come through for you, always and forever.

Deuteronomy 31:8

"The Lord himself goes before you and will be with you; he will *never* leave you nor forsake you. Do not be afraid; do not be discouraged."

Psalm 73:23-26

Yet I am *always* with you; you hold me by my right hand. You guide me with your counsel, and afterward you will take me into glory. Whom have I in heaven but you? And earth has nothing I desire besides you. My flesh and my heart may fail, but God is the strength of my heart and my portion *forever.*"

Psalm 103:2-6

"Praise the Lord, my soul, and forget not all his benefits— who forgives *all* your sins and heals *all* your diseases, who redeems your life from the pit and crowns you with love and compassion, who satisfies your desires with good things so that your youth is renewed like the eagle's. The Lord works for righteousness and justice for *all* the oppressed."

Psalm 118:29

"Give thanks to the Lord, for he is good; his love endures *forever*."

Lamentations 3:22-24

"Because of the Lord's great love we are not consumed, for his compassions *never* fail. They are new *every* morning; great is your faithfulness. I say to myself, "The Lord is my portion, therefore I will wait for him.""

Isaiah 40:8

"The grass withers and flowers fade, but the word of our God stands *forever*."

Isaiah 40:28 NLT

"The Lord is the everlasting God, the Creator of *all* the earth. He *never* grows weak or weary. *No one* can measure the depths of his understanding."

Isaiah 43:13 NLT

"From eternity to eternity I am God. *No one* can snatch *anyone* out of my hand. *No one* can undo what I have done."

Matthew 6:33 NLT

"Seek the Kingdom of God above all else, and live righteously, and he will give you *everything* you need."

Matthew 28:20

"And surely I am with you *always*, to the very end of the age."

Matthew 24:35; Mark 13:31; Luke 21:33

"Heaven and earth will pass away, but my words will *never* pass away."

John 3:16

"For God so loved the world that he gave his one and only Son, that whoever believes in him shall not perish but have *eternal* life."

John 6:35, 37

Then Jesus declared, "I am the bread of life. Whoever comes to me will *never* go hungry, and whoever believes in me will *never* be thirsty...*All* those the Father gives me will come to me, and whoever comes to me I will *never* drive away."

Romans 8:28

"And we know that in *all* things God works for the good of those who love him, who have been called according to his purpose."

Romans 8:37-39

"No, in *all* these things we are more than conquerors through him who loved us. For I am convinced that neither death nor life, neither angels nor demons, neither the present nor the future, nor any powers, neither height nor depth, nor *anything* else in all creation, will be able to separate us from the love of God that is in Christ Jesus our Lord."

1 Corinthians 13:7-8

"Love *always* protects, *always* trusts, *always* hopes, *always* perseveres… Love *never* fails.

1 Peter 1:23 NLT

"For you have been born again, but not to a life that will quickly end. Your new life will last *forever* because it comes from the *eternal*, living word of God."

Hebrews 13:8

"Jesus Christ is the same yesterday and today and *forever*."

Revelation 21:3-5

"And I heard a loud voice from the throne saying, "Look! God's dwelling place is now among the people, and he will dwell with them. They will be his people, and God himself will be with them and be their God. He will wipe *every* tear from their eyes. There will be no more death or mourning or crying or pain, for the old order of things has passed away. He who was seated on the throne said, "I am making *everything* new!" Then he said, "Write this down, for these words are trustworthy and true."

ACKNOWLEDGEMENTS

Kimberly, thank you for gently showing me that I can do this. You keep showing up, you teach me strength and kindness and perseverance, and you lead me closer to Christ with each conversation.

Hannah, thank you for lending your expertise to this project. Your creativity and talent in design is evident. Beyond the arts, you have an incredible gift for hospitality. Thank you for the privilege of witnessing this gift on display for the past three years.

Beth, thank you for walking with me through the past year and for your support in editing this book. Through the highs and the lows, you welcomed me, allowed me space to work through hard things, and reminded me of who I am in Christ.

Diane, thank you for believing in me and this book enough to write the foreword. I'm grateful to have met you and for the way your choosing to start 4word gifted me a community I didn't know I needed. Also, thank you again for the bunt cake in Dallas (I will never forget)!

To the women who graciously offered their hard-earned wisdom to us all, I am grateful for your partnership, and I am grateful for your faithfulness in your work as your ministry. You each inspire, encourage, and lead us well in learning how to build our lives on Christ. You all are a living testimony of Colossians 2:6-7. May we follow in your footsteps.

Jordan, thank you for being an editor extraordinaire. I'm so glad to have met you through 4word. You made this book better.

My friends, thanks for the laughs, the lessons, and the late night memories. Knowing each of you has taught me the power of compassion, the need for community, and the art of full-laughs. You're my people, so you're stuck with me.

Last but not least: to my parents, thank you doesn't begin to cover it. You gave me the gift of growing up knowing Jesus, you love sacrificially, and you continue to support me even when I have crazy ideas like writing a book. I am blessed to be your daughter.

AS YOU GROW UP LETTERS BIOS

Patty Ross

Patty Ross is an accomplished Senior Executive who leverages her experience, leadership acuity, and definitive record, positioning her as a go-to global strategist in the consumer product industry. Patty most recently served Apple as an Executive Advisor for the People organization, where she delivered talent management, retention, inclusion, and diversity strategies across all US and global divisions. Patty spent the majority of her career with Nike, where she dedicated over 34 years in strategy, process-re-engineering, operations, and general management roles. Including GM, Asia Pacific Equipment & Operations; Senior Director, Global Footwear; VP, Global Product Process Innovation, and finally VP, Global Operations & Technology.

Patty is routinely trusted and relied upon to start up new divisions, functional units, and incubators, charged with implementing change, innovation, and growth, and her direct efforts led to millions of revenue dollars for Nike annually. In addition to her professional contributions at Nike, Patty gained a reputation for both innovative excellence and reliable execution by spearheading value initiatives such as the first e-commerce B2B website for retailers, Nike's Product Creation Center of Excellence, Nike's Workplace of the Future, and the Women of Nike Diversity Network.

Patty holds a Bachelor of Applied Science degree in Finance and Marketing from Portland State University, a coaching certification in Executive Leadership Development from The Hudson Institute of Coaching, and an Advanced Management certificate in Business Administration and General Management from Harvard Business School. She is also a graduate of the Executive Education Program at Harvard Business School, where she focused on corporate boards, governance, operations, and management.

In addition to growing and reshaping organizations as a strategic advisor and operations leader, Patty is also active in a variety of professional boards and speaking engagements. She serves as a Board Member for Nautilus, Inc., MMC Corp, 4word, and an Advisor to a Fortune 50 Executive. Patty is also an active member of NACD, The Athena Alliance, WomenExecs on Boards and Women Corporate Directors, where she is committed to the professional development of executives of all ages.

Emily Lan

Emily earned a BBA in Accounting from the University of Alaska Fairbanks and began her career in the Big 4 with KPMG. After spending a number of years in audit and corporate accounting, she transitioned to agency recruiting. And in 2020, she completed a M.A. in Creative Writing at Wilkes University. She lives in Dallas with her husband, daughter, and pup.

Shea Davis

Shea Davis has over 25 years of experience as a tax, accounting and finance expert advising companies in complex situations. She is a strategic networker and advisor with a unique blend of Wall Street Investment Banking, Big Four Accounting, professional tax experience including Internal Revenue Service, and project finance structuring. Shea has served on multiple Boards and has held officer positions with many more not-for-profit organizations. Operational and financial acumen coupled with strong relationship building skills.

Brianna Morton

Brianna Morton is the College Access Counselor at Riverside High School in Decatur County, Tennessee. Brianna worked in the counseling field as a mental health counselor for 4 years and a clinical supervisor for 1 year. Brianna joined the Ayers Foundation in November 2011.

She graduated from the University of North Alabama with a major in Psychology and double minor in Criminal Justice and Spanish. She also obtained a Masters degree from the University of North Alabama in Community Counseling where she also worked as the Graduate Assistant for the Counselor Education Department.

Pat Asp

Patricia is an accomplished C-Suite Executive and Board Member who leverages her experience, leadership acuity and decisive record positioning her as an expert in organizational and digital transformational, innovation, and scaling multi-location distributed model businesses for strategic and financial performance improvement. Through her unparalleled experience in aligning Purpose, People, Process and Profit, she uses proven methodologies for performance amplification, by integrating values into business models. She is passionate about using her experience to serve executives with their strategic intention, personal and company growth, problem solving, or experience enhancement while enriching the human spirit environment by focusing on the strengths for the betterment of the individual and the organization. She currently assists clients wit performance enhancement, strategic planning, executive coaching and development, and transforming and codifying company cultures in diverse environments for sustainability, exit strategy planning, or with project areas that have been designated in need of priority focus. Patricia has significant business, culture and team transformational experience with companies ranging in size from start-ups to $7 Billion in revenue in a wide range of sectors including healthcare, education, business and industry, consumer services, and pre-school photography. As the Chief Executive Officer and Board Director of a national photography company, she led the strategic digital transformation design for this private equity company to improve cash flow, quality of earnings, and positioned for an optimal exit event, as well as leading the transition from Founder-led while enhancing the customer experience competitively.

Patricia was an executive for 25 years with The ServiceMaster Company, a Fortune 500 global service company voted the most respected company in the world by Financial Times. ServiceMaster was comprised of 5,000 contract management, franchise and company-owned global locations that were grown organically and through significant acquisition including Terminix, TruGreen ChemLawn, ARS/Rescue Rooter, Merry Maids, American Home Shield, and Furniture Medic and subsequent rollups and integration targets. She led Performance Improvement, Human Resources, Strategic Planning & Development, Hospitality Services, Strategic Program Development, and served as President of Food Management Services. During her tenure she reported directly to the chairman and vice chairman, and led the first Six Sigma launch and implementation that encompassed a $4 Billion, distributed-model, multiple-location, global service company, recovering $15M investment in first year (shareholder neutral), and creating $60 million savings / 5-6 cents per share in year two. Additionally, she was on the executive team that strategically positioned and divested the contract management division, exceeding the forecasted purchase price, designed and implemented an interactive strategic planning process that was cross-functional and cross-business units, and developed new customer-centered strategies for this distributed model company.

Additionally, she served as President & Chief Operations Officer of a for-profit education company leading the financial turnaround during a dramatic economic downturn of the education market. The transformation included a strategic repositioning from the legacy business to a charter school business model and successfully opened 10 charter schools, exceeding budgets, enrollment and financial proformas and achieving SACS accreditation for all schools. She has served on both for profit and not for profit boards. Patricia currently serves as President and Senior Adviser at Compass Executives – Nashville Management Group, Inc., as an Independent Director of 4word, founded to help women reach their God-given potential with confidence and as Advisory Board Director and Chair of Generate.

Christa Vanzant

Christa's career at JCI began over 19 years ago and has expanded into business & executive coaching for Johnson Controls. She is a learning manager and coach to JCI's internal teams as well as external JCI channel partners in the areas of business and professional leadership.

Christa is a graduate of the University of Oklahoma with a BA in Organizational Leadership. Before her long-standing career with JCI, she worked for AT&T and helped launch a successful small business with her husband while raising her family. Christa spent many years consulting & coaching teams & small businesses. She is currently the lead business instructor & coach for JCI's Ducted Systems Academy. Many of her workshops center on leadership & professional development, including mentorship & coaching.

Her heart is to help teams and leaders at all levels develop better communication and higher levels of emotional intelligence to lead with the foundation of trust. Christa has been the keynote speaker and workshop leader for small business & industry events. Her certifications include Franklin Covey Leadership, DDI Global Leadership, MillerHeiman/Korn Ferry International.

Christa is a local chapter leader for 4WordWomen.org, OKC, and has participated in 4Words mentorship program. Additionally, she conducts workshops for single women & mothers to help them develop professionally to enhance their careers & improve their financial position to have a better quality of life.

Simi John

Simi was born in India and moved to Dallas, TX at the age of 7. She graduated with her doctorate in physical therapy and got married to her best friend Jayson in 2010. They live in Oklahoma and have 2 kids.

Simi loves to equip women to know who they are and live faithfully right where they are! Simi is a speaker and author of "I Am Not: Break Free From Stereotypes & Become The Woman God Made You To Be" (available on Amazon)

You can connect with her on Instagram: @simijohn

Heidi Rasmussen

Communicator. Brand Builder. Trainer. Strategic Planner. Organizer. Customer Service Advocate. Team Builder. UX defender. Writer. Mentor. Coffee Addict. Overall: gettin' stuff done and makin' it happen.

After 27 years in the retail industry, Heidi took on a new challenge. From corporate life to entrepreneurship. From fashion retail to the employee benefits industry. At 15 years old, Heidi started at

JCPenney where she went from a sales floor associate to Divisional Vice President at the corporate office & led the largest brand launch in JCPenney history.

In her current role as a co-founder and COO, she launched freshbenies (as in, a fresh approach to benefits) to give employers and their employees practical tools to control their healthcare dime, time and peace of mind.

freshbenies has been named to the Inc. 5000 list of fastest growing companies in America four consecutive years and the Dallas 100 two consecutive years. freshbenies also received two Health Value Awards given to companies that are dedicated to providing innovative, value-based healthcare.

No matter what the product or service, Heidi has learned that people want brands that engage and help simplify life. Even more, they want brands to follow through on that promise. That's what she does.

Kimberly MacNeill

Kimberly MacNeill seeks to be a unique, creative, spiritual voice in the world inspiring others to love God, walk in faith, and do good. A licensed minister, she has served professionally on staff at local churches and traveled speaking around the United States for 26 years. She holds a degree in English and a Master of Divinity and is the author of Whispers: Transforming Words For Your Ever-Changing Life. You can learn more about her work at theinspirationlounge.org. She and her husband Dave reside in the High Country of North Carolina.

LaTonya Hockett

LaTonya Hockett is a finance director by trade, but an avid encourager when it comes to speaking about waiting. She knows what it takes to wait. She and her husband, Chip (of 13+ years) has been believing God for children for 11 years.

She was born and raised in Covington, TN, but has lived in Nashville, TN for almost 24 years. She lives by the scripture Isaiah 40:31, "But those who trust in the Lord will find new strength. They will soar high on wings like eagles. They will run and not grow weary. They will walk and not faint."

In her spare time, she loves to relax at home watching a good movie or investigative TV shows! She also loves to dance and plan events.

D. Michelle Thompson

D. Michelle Thompson has twenty years' experience in Advertising and Marketing. Michelle's diverse background includes working for top advertising agencies managing budgets from $100 Million to $500 Million for clients such as Kellogg's, Tropicana, and Got Milk? She then honed her Brand Management skills managing the $2 Billion dollar Bounty® brand while at Procter & Gamble.

In June 2009, Michelle left her comfortable salary at Procter & Gamble to focus full-time on her own purpose/calling as a writer, speaker and consultant. Since that time, she remains based in Cincinnati while traveling on assignment with her own firm, Destiny Resets shaped by a mission to "empower leadership ripe for a healthy workplace." This work led Michelle to Dubai where she facilitated Sales/Marketing training for a room full of Middle Eastern executives in 2013.

Michelle launched her podcast "You Belong" in October 2019 on on iTunes and Podbean to empower professionals to push past the desire to "fit in, even when you don't" combining inspirational nuggets and practical tips for work and life. To date, she has authored three books, with the fourth, You Belong coming soon. Today, she also leads an initiative entitled "Courageous Love at Work" challenging leaders to move from being "color blind" to "color brave" with a model for racial reconciliation in the workplace.

Visit her websites www.destinyresets.com for more information.

Susan Tolles

Susan Tolles is passionate about helping women flourish by inspiring and equipping them to live according to God's purpose for their lives. Susan's life's journey has taken her from being a career woman to a rich experience as a stay-at-home mom, then to becoming a first-time entrepreneur at 53. As a Certified Christian Life Purpose Coach and author, she has been a guide, strategist, and cheerleader for women around the world who desire to live with deeper meaning, less stress, and greater joy in God's calling. Susan currently serves at the Director of Community Groups at 4word, a global ministry that serves Christian women in the workplace, supporting hundreds of women so they can achieve their God-given potential with confidence. She and her husband Jim live in Austin, Texas surrounded by three grown children and their families who light up their lives.

Kelli Henley

Kelli Henley earned her bachelor's degree in Accounting from Middle Tennessee State University and later completed her MBA at Belmont University in Nashville, TN. She has 10+ years of experience in public accounting with a specialization in tax and now works in the tax department of a large, national healthcare group. Through managing and developing young talent while in public accounting, she realized her passion for coaching and teaching others and now serves as an adjunct accounting professor at her alma mater, MTSU, and a health and fitness coach focused on pointing women to Jesus Christ, our Lord and Savior. She currently sits on the board of directors for Girls on the Run of Middle Tennessee and volunteers as a small group leader for junior high girls at her church. She and her husband Jamey have been married for just over 7 years and reside in Murfreesboro, TN with their ferret, Meiko. They enjoy traveling and cheering on the Nashville Predators together and are self-proclaimed adrenaline junkies.

ENDNOTES

CHAPTER 0

1. There is no shame in asking for help. If you struggle with anxiety or depression, know that you are not alone and there are people who want to help you. Beyond your immediate friends and family, you can call the National Suicide Prevention Lifeline at 1-800-273-8255 (TALK), The Samaritans at (877) 870-4673 (HOPE), or reach out to a local church to talk with a pastor in your area.

2. Bethany Dillon, "Hallelujah." Imagination, 2005.

CHAPTER 1

3. Exodus 4:13 NLT

4. Exodus 33:15 NLT

5. Warren Wiersbe, The Wiersbe Bible Commentary: Old Testament 2nd ed. (Colorado Springs, CO: David C Cook, 2007), 150.

6. To read more of the story of Moses starting his journey, go to Exodus 3 and 4.

7. See John 21:15-17

CHAPTER 2

8. Erin Davis, She Reads Truth Bible, "Sing to the Lord," General editor, Raechel Myers, Ed.; Full rev. ed. (Nashville: Holman Bible Publishers, 2017), 104.

9. See Matthew 25:14-30 NLT

10. A.W. Tozer, The Pursuit of God (Camp Hill, PA: Christian Publications, 1982), ch 10.

CHAPTER 3

11. See Matthew 28:19

12. Diane Paddison , Work, Love, Pray (Grand Rapids: Zondervan, 2011), 122.

13. Matthew 28:19 NLT

14. Philippians 1:27 CSB

15. See Hebrews 12:1

CHAPTER 4

16. Mark Batterson, The Circle Maker (Grand Rapids: Zondervan, 2011), 79.

17. Esther 4:14 NLT

18. Louie Giglio, Goliath Must Fall: Winning the Battle Against Your Giants (Nashville: W Publishing Group, 2017), ch 4.

19. Romans 12:3,6 NLT

20. Galatians 6:4 NLT

21. Bob Goff, @bobgoff. "We won't be distracted by comparison if we are captivated by purpose." Twitter. Nov 28, 2014. https://twitter.com/bobgoff/status/538346879474749441

CHAPTER 5

22. See Jeremiah 31:33, Deuteronomy 6:6, or Proverbs 7:3

23. Psalm 23 NLT

24. Psalm 37:34 NLT

25. Psalm 23:3 NLT

CHAPTER 6

26. If you're not convinced of these statements, I encourage you to read through these scripture verses: John 1:12, 3:16-17; Acts 2:21; Romans 8:17,35-39, 15:7; Galatians 4:6-7; 1 John 4:10

27. You know, the moment the man runs into the woman and she spills her coffee all over her outfit. It's the moment they meet, and it's usually cute and sets the stage for their happily-ever-after.

28. Tim Keller, Every Good Endeveavor (New York: Dutton, 2012), 74.

29. See Philippians 3:8

30. Tozer, The Pursuit of God, preface.

CHAPTER 7

31. I'm including a picture of my actual blanket in case you don't believe me:

32. Stuart Townend & Keith Getty, "In Christ Alone." Thankyou Music, 2001

33. Edward Mote, "My Hope is Built on Nothing Less." 1834

34. See 1 Peter 1:25 or Isaiah 40:8

CHAPTER 8

35. See Romans 3:23

36. See Matthew 7:3-5

37. 1 Corinthians 12:4-6 NIV

38. 1 Corinthians 12:31 NLT

39. See 1 Corinthians 13

40. "Pepé Le Pew." Wikipedia: The Free Encyclopedia, Wikimedia Foundation, 22 February 2021, 01:16, en.wikipedia.org/wiki/ Pep%C3%A9_Le_Pew. Accessed 27 February 2021.

41. See Lamentations 3:23

42. See Romans 8:37-39

43. See 2 Corinthians 3:17

44. See 1 Corinthians 8:3; Isaiah 43:1

45. See Isaiah 49:16

46. See Romans 6:5-11

47. See Ephesians 2:8

48. Carey Scott, Uncommon: Pursuing a Life of Passion and Purpose (Uhrichsville, OH: Shiloh Run Press, 2017), ch 2.

CHAPTER 9

49. See Romans 8:28

50. Courtney Watson. "when the fear comes." Faithful Fireworks, 3 March 2019, www.courtneygracewrites.com/post/when-the-fear-comes.

51. Psalm 91: 1-7.14-16 NLT

52. Exodus 17:15 NLT

53. See Colossians 3:7-11

54. See 2 Corinthians 1:20

55. Jonah 1:3 NLT

56. Jonah 3:1-3 NLT

CHAPTER 10

57. For the record: literally zero part of this plan actually happened, and I can't thank God enough for it.

58. See Ephesians 3:20-21

59. See Psalm 139:16

CHAPTER 11

60. Proverbs 16:9 NIV

61. Proverbs 19:21 NIV

62. See Proverbs 4:23

63. "Garth Brooks." Saturday Night Live, directed by Beth McCarthy-Miller, performance by Cheri Oteri, season 25, episode 5, NBC Studios, 1999

64. 2 Fast 2 Furious. Directed by John Singleton, performance by Tyrese Gibson, 2003

65. Tozer, The Pursuit of God, ch 8.

66. John 5:19,30 CSB

67. 2 Corinthians 12:9-10 NLT

68. Elizabeth George, A Woman After God's Own Heart (Eugene, OR: Harvest House, 2006), 18.

69. See Proverbs 3:5-6

70. See Proverbs 16:3

71. See Ecclesiastes 3:11

72. See Matthew 7:7-8

73. To read more about Noah, read Genesis 6-8

CHAPTER 12

74. Ephesians 4:4-7,16 NLT

75. 1 Corinthians 12:26-27 NLT

76. 1 John 4:18 ESV

77. Bob Goff, Everybody, Always (Nashville, TN: Nelson Books, 2018), 92.

78. See Luke 5:17-26

79. Luke 5:20 NLT

CHAPTER 13

80. See Psalm 139:5

81. See John 17:24

82. See 1 John 3:1

83. Scc Romans 12:2

84. See Colossians 3:17 or Philippians 2:13

EPILOGUE

All verses are from the NIV Bible except where specified with the verse. Emphasis added.

CONNECT WITH COURTNEY

Find her and her **Faithful Fireworks** blog online
at www.courtneygracewrites.com

> **Faithful Fireworks** blogs are an extension of this book.
> They are lessons learned, precious reminders from the Lord,
> and insight into life as we let our faith guide our work.

Subscribe to her **Made for Monday** emails
at www.courtneygracewrites.com/join-us

> **Made for Monday** emails are for the weary worker who
> needs a reminder every Monday morning that you are made
> to work with God. It's a short reminder for our hearts and
> minds to refocus on the God who establishes the work of our
> hands as we begin another week.

Follow her on socials for day-to-day inspiration and encouragement
and the occasional pictures of hockey games and Christmas trees.

> Instagram: @courtneygracewrites

> Facebook: @courtneygracewrites

Courtney Grace
W R I T E S *

CPSIA information can be obtained
at www.ICGtesting.com
Printed in the USA
JSHW042100210421
13760JS00002B/8